On Original Sin and *A Disputation with the Jew, Leo, Concerning the Advent of Christ, the Son of God*

ON ORIGINAL SIN

and

A DISPUTATION
WITH THE
JEW, LEO, CONCERNING THE ADVENT OF CHRIST, THE SON OF GOD

Two Theological Treatises

ODO OF TOURNAI

Translated with an introduction and notes by
IRVEN M. RESNICK

University of Pennsylvania Press

Philadelphia

Library of Congress Cataloging-in-Publication Data
Odo, of Tournai, ca. 1060–1113.
    [De peccato originali. English]
    On original sin ; and, A disputation with the Jew, Leo, concerning the Advent of Christ, the Son of God : two theological treatises / Odo of Tournai ; translated with an introduction and notes by Irven M. Resnick.
        p. cm. — (University of Pennsylvania Press Middle Ages series)
    Includes bibliographical references and index.
    ISBN 0–8122–3288–7. — ISBN (invalid) 0–8122–1540–0 (pbk.)
    1. Sin, Original—Early works to 1800. 2. Judaism—Controversial literature—Early works to 1800. 3. Apologetics—Early works to 1800. 4. Judaism (Christian theology)—Early works to 1800. I. Resnick, Irven Michael. II. Odo, of Tournai, ca. 1060–1113. Disputatio contra Judaeum Leonem nomine de adventu Christi filii Dei. English.
III. Title: On original sin. IV. Title: Disputation with the Jew, Leo, concerning the Advent of Christ, the Son of God. V. Series: Middle Ages series.
BT720.O36 1994
233'.14—dc20   94-16217
                                                                                      CIP

Permission is acknowledged to reprint previously published material as follows:

Irven M. Resnick, "Odo of Tournai's *De peccato originali* and the Problem of Original Sin," *Medieval Philosophy and Theology, volume I,* edited by Mark D. Jordan. Copyright © 1991 by the University of Notre Dame Press. Used by permission.

Cover: Reprinted from Avril Henry, editor: *Biblia Pauperum: A Facsimile of the Forty-Page Blockbook.* Copyright © 1987 by Cornell University. Used by permission of the publisher, Cornell University Press.

Contents

Acknowledgments

A historical study and translation inevitably owes much to a number of individual scholars who were kind enough to answer my inquiries or correct errors I might otherwise have made. While I cannot name them all, I would be remiss if I failed to mention some of those without whose support or assistance this project would have been a much more difficult undertaking. First, I should like to thank the librarians at Harvard University's Houghton Library for providing access to its manuscript collection. I would also like to thank librarians at the Institut de Recherche et d'Histoire des Textes at the Centre National de la Recherche Scientifique in Paris for supplying manuscripts of Odo's work in microfilm copies and for correcting at least one entry in the manuscript catalogues. Dr. Albert Houssiau, Bishop of Liège, also provided help with the manuscript tradition and directed me to Mr. Naedenoen's dissertation on Odo's *Exposition on the Canon of the Mass*, submitted to the University of Louvain. I should also like to thank Charles Dereine, whose work first brought Odo of Tournai to my attention. Despite a long illness, Dr. Dereine was kind enough to provide me with additional information on manuscripts at the abbey of Marchiennes.

Professors Kenneth Kitchell at Louisiana State University and Gerald Press at Hunter College read at least portions of the translation and offered suggestions or corrections. So too did Professor Ann Matter for the University of Pennsylvania Press. I am grateful for their comments and for those of other readers.

I must also thank the National Endowment for the Humanities, which provided me with a Travel to Collections Grant to support my research, and the Littauer Foundation, whose financial assistance helped bring this volume to press.

Lastly, let me thank my wife, Elizabeth, who listened patiently to the many frustrations that accompanied this project, and our daughter, Ariel, who is a visible reminder of the perfection that animates the religious quest. For whatever imperfections remain in this work, however, I am alone responsible.

Abbreviations

CCSL	*Corpus Christianorum, Series Latina*
CCCM	*Corpus Christianorum, Continuatio Medievalis*
CSEL	*Corpus Scriptorum Ecclesiasticorum Latinorum*
MGH, SS	*Monumenta Germaniae Historica, Scriptores*
PL	*Patrologiae Cursus Completus, Series Latina*
(B)	*Maxima bibliotheca veterum Patrum*
(D)	Douai bibl. mun. 201 (12th C.)
(J)	Harvard MS Judaica 16 (15th C.)
(M)	J.P. Migne's *Patrologiae Cursus Completus, Series Latina*, vol. 160: 1071–1112
(T)	Troyes Bibl. mun. 398 (12th C.)

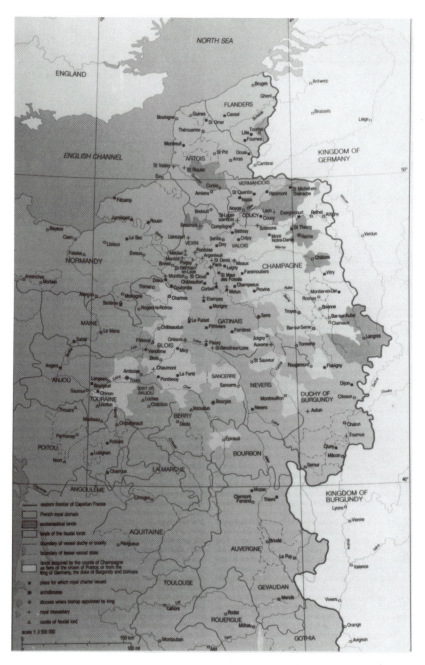

Capetian France, ca. AD 1100. Reproduced by permission of Andromeda Oxford, Ltd.

Introduction: Odo of Tournai

Tournai at the End of the Eleventh Century

Odo of Tournai (d. 1113) — or, sometimes, Odo of Cambrai or Odo of Orléans — was born soon after A.D. 1060 in Orléans, during the reign of King Philip I of France. While still a young man in his twenties Odo's career flourished as a secular master (*magister*) at the cathedral schools of Toul and Tournai. Later, he embarked upon the religious life, first as a canon of St. Augustine and then as the first abbot of the restored monastery of St. Martin of Tournai. At the conclusion of his brief but distinguished ecclesiastical career, he ascended the episcopal throne as Bishop of Cambrai (1105–1113). These positions not only placed Odo in contact with important persons and events during a troubled period in the history of Empire and Church, but also provided for him access to new intellectual currents of the day. Here he was not merely a passive recipient of new ideas, but was himself a contributor to the cultural flowering that marks the renaissance of the twelfth century.[1]

Regrettably, we know very little about Odo prior to his arrival at Tournai in the 1080s. We are largely dependent upon two contemporary — or nearly contemporary — sources for our information: the *Liber restaurationis Sancti Martini Tornacensis*, which was written between 1142 and 1146 by Herman, third abbot of the monastery of St. Martin of Tournai;[2] and a work entitled *De Odonis episcopi Cameracensis vita vel moribus*,[3] written by Amand du Chastel (Amandus de Castello). Amand was received at St. Martin's in 1095 by Odo and later became prior at Anchin (*Aquicinctinus*), where Odo died in 1113. Herman's history, although written three decades after Odo's death, is nevertheless the more complete and more important of these two sources. Herman's father, Radulf, and his mother, Mainsend, came from the knightly class. Radulf and his four young sons entered the monastery of St. Martin of Tournai during Odo's abbacy. His wife, Mainsend, a powerful and wealthy woman, was likewise received into the religious life by Odo, and entered a monastic foundation he established nearby for some sixty women.[4] Herman, the third son, was educated by Odo himself.[5] Although younger than Amand du Chastel, Herman was in a good position to witness events that affected Odo, the monastery, and the entire region surrounding Tournai.[6]

Odo's parents were Gerard and Cecelia of Orléans.[7] Since as a young man Odo acquired a reputation as a teacher and scholar learned in grammar, rhetoric, and dialectic (the *trivium*),[8] one may assume that he received a good education. He first taught at Toul, and then was called to Tournai by the canons of the cathedral of Notre-Dame.[9] Odo taught for five years at the cathedral school, where his reputation attracted students from France, Flanders, Normandy, Italy, Saxony, and Burgundy.[10]

Artifacts found in Tournai from the first through fourth centuries attest that it was settled during Roman times, making Tournai one of the most ancient settlements in the region.[11] It was evangelized in the third century by St. Piat, and served as a capital city for the Salian Franks from 431 to 440. Under the Merovingians, it lost its royal status. But the Merovingian King, Clovis, compensated Tournai for its loss of rank by endowing it as an episcopal see which the metropolitan of Reims, St. Remi, conferred upon St. Eleutherius (ca. 497–500). From the sixth century, the bishops there fulfilled de facto if not de jure the functions of counts palatine, representing the king of the Franks. In the second half of the ninth century Tournai was attached to the county of Flanders, and the episcopal see at Tournai was joined to Noyon to create a single diocese. This union continued until 1146, when Tournai was established as an independent see.[12] Yet prior to this, despite the Norman invasions and a deterioration in the quality of religious life among the canons and clerks in Tournai, the power of the bishop of Noyon-Tournai and the cathedral chapter at Notre Dame had grown during the ninth and tenth centuries.

It was at Tournai — an ancient Roman settlement and powerful episcopal see — that Odo arrived in the 1080s. His arrival coincided with tremendous economic growth and prosperity for Tournai. In 1052 the city had received a communal charter from Baudouin V of Lille. In 1092 it created its great market fair and attracted thousands annually to its popular religious procession honoring the Virgin Mary (*Notre-Dame flamande*), a procession originated by Bishop Rabod II of Tournai in order to bring to an end an epidemic that had decimated the region. In order to avert God's wrath, the bishop gathered the people at the cathedral of Notre Dame and imposed a penitential discipline, cut off the hair of the young people, and insisted on fasts, vigils, and a barefoot procession circling the city to deliver alms and pledges to the saints. But after the epidemic abated what had begun as a penitential observance was transformed into an occasion for celebration. Herman confides that the annual autumn procession was re-enacted in his own day, but that its character had changed: it attracted as many as 100,000 celebrants, of both sexes, more interested in horse racing and games than religion.[13]

While the religious character of the procession may have deteriorated, its economic impact grew. It attracted pilgrims, trade, and commerce to Tournai. Equally important, the events that led Rabod II to order the procession gave a prominent role to the poor church of St. Martin of Tournai, whose restoration was linked to the disease that afflicted so many in the area. The sick, who suffered from an illness that rendered them especially malodorous, were initially carried to the cathedral of Notre Dame, where they hoped Mary would herself heal them. But when the church was crowded with the infirm, the canons were repulsed by their awful stench and cast them out. In the same way, every parish church around Tournai rejected those afflicted with the disease (which was commonly called "hell's fire," in part, it seems, because the infirm were marked with the odor of burned flesh). In the end, the sick were brought to the church of St. Martin of Tournai, which had been ravaged and almost entirely destroyed by the Normans (ca. 850–880). St. Martin's was so poor that it did not even have a priest. A priest from a nearby church dedicated to St. Piat would visit, but only to bury the dead. When the epidemic abated, presumably due to the efforts on high of St. Martin himself, the elders of the city called on the bishop to restore the church and to return to it the lands and income it had once held, which the bishop had conferred as a benefice on powerful noble families. The penitential procession, then, which was believed to have ended the epidemic, brought great economic growth and prosperity. This prosperity expanded the Cathedral of Notre Dame, brought a brief flowering of intellectual and artistic life to Tournai, and ultimately restored St. Martin's.

Philosophical Debate at Tournai

Odo had originally come to Tournai in order to teach at the cathedral school and to participate in this cultural flowering. His lectures attracted so many that Tournai at that time has been described as a "little Athens."[14] Odo's lectures addressed questions in astronomy and natural science[15] and treated traditional philosophical concerns, for example the tension between the doctrines of divine foreknowledge and human freedom explored in Boethius's *Consolation of Philosophy*.[16] These lectures also plunged Odo into the most intense philosophical debate to emerge in this period, concerning the status of universals.

The debate over universals, which had attracted the interest of thinkers during the Carolingian age, expanded with seemingly explosive force among Odo's generation of early Scholastic philosophers. A tenth-century marginal gloss to the *Ten Categories* of Pseudo-Augustine seems to provide evidence already of a growing skepticism regarding the doctrine of universals inherited from pagan and Christian authorities[17] and to demonstrate the growing appeal of a position that will later come to be identified with the nominalists.

The term *nominales* or nominalists is not attested until the late twelfth or early thirteenth century. Nominalism is therefore a term applied retrospectively to a group of authors before the twelfth century who share a certain skepticism toward the received Platonic intellectual inheritance, especially with respect to the status of universals. The term is more commonly applied to a group of thinkers from the late thirteenth and fourteenth centuries, including William of Ockham, Robert Holcot, and others. To the extent that pre-Scholastic or early Scholastic thinkers were engaged in a debate about the nature or status of universals bearing some similarity to later debate, it may not be inappropriate to refer to them too as nominalists, once we recognize that contemporaries were unfamiliar with the name,[18] and that the abstract and sometimes inflexible categories of nominalist and realist are conceptions of historians of philosophy that do not apply neatly, as Marenbon cautions, to any philosopher of the early Middle Ages.[19]

With this caveat in mind, one may yet acknowledge that issues important to the nominalist and realist debate were treated by early Scholastic thinkers, including Odo himself and Odo's brilliant but difficult younger contemporary, Peter Abelard.[20] On one level, the conflict concerned the competing authority of the philosophers of antiquity and their medieval disciples. It was increasingly clear that Plato and Aristotle disagreed on the nature of universals, despite continuing efforts to harmonize their positions. As early as the end of the tenth century, this sense that Plato and Aristotle disagreed regarding the reality of universals, thereby creating a conflict for those who would consider themselves their disciples, disturbed the Italian monk Gunzo. In a piece of controversial literature stemming from his visit to the monastery of St. Gall, Gunzo notes that Boethius has shown that Aristotle denied that the five predicables or universals (genus, species, difference, property, and accident) subsist in themselves, while Plato insists that they are independent and subsistent things. In a reflection of the consternation many must have felt when they considered this problem, Gunzo asks frankly which one is to be believed, when the authority of each is unimpeachable?[21]

This recognition that the authority of the ancients was in conflict on a fundamental point of their metaphysics signaled the beginning of the controversy over the nature of universals. In brief, this question of universals asks whether our general ideas or conceptions, which can be predicated of many individual and distinct objects — as "man" can be predicated of Socrates, Aristotle, and others — have any *objective* value. That is, do they refer only to a subjective creation of the mind, perhaps serving merely as convenient categories for ordering our sense experience of individuals, or do they correspond to objective realities? For example, when I contemplate a universal — say, triangles in general — and assert that every triangle is defined by three interior angles equal to 180 degrees, am I only making an assertion about a certain logical relationship between triangles and their constituent angles, or is my assertion also objectively valid in the extramental world? Does this statement express not only a logical truth but also an ontological truth, one valid not only for *thought* but also for *being*?

While over the next several centuries diverse answers to these questions would increase in number, at the end of the eleventh century the issue was beginning to be explored with great intensity. In the sixth century, Boethius had raised these questions in his second commentary on Porphyry's *Isagoge*, a commentary which, manuscript evidence suggests, enjoyed a growing reading audience from the tenth century. Although Boethius recognized the differences between Platonic and Aristotelian traditions, he nevertheless failed to render a judgment over which approach was correct.[22] Yet his own evident preference for the Platonic solution found in his *Consolation of Philosophy* had helped establish it as the most widely accepted philosophical opinion. This position, usually identified as exaggerated realism (in order to distinguish it from the so-called modified realism espoused in the thirteenth century by Thomas Aquinas) tended to accept that the universal as such exists in reality in a manner closely corresponding to our universal idea, not only with respect to the content or form of that idea but also in the manner in which that idea is represented in the mind. Thus, because the universal idea — horse, dog, and so forth — is represented in the mind apart from any *particular* horse or dog of our actual experience; because it is contemplated apart from matter and the changes wrought by time, and because it is predicable of many individuals of our experience, there must exist *in reality* a universal object that enjoys the perfection of the idea. Where these universals exist and how we obtain our understanding of them are further questions, but these only become pressing once one has addressed a more central concern: namely, do universals exist?

When Odo was teaching at Tournai, he followed the teaching of the ancients (*antiqui*)[23] who, he surmised, had argued that universals exist in reality, in the objective order (*in re*) and not merely as terms or words *we* use to help us order the painfully discrete and individual objects of experience. His contemporaries who challenged the teaching of the ancient authorities on the nature of universals were perceived to be equating the universal with a mere linguistic device. For this reason, they were often castigated for reducing the universal, the genus or class name, to nothing more than a *common name* established by convention for things which are themselves individual, which led to their association with later nominalists. For these, then, universals do not exist in the objective order (*in re*) but only in the linguistic order or in the order of thought given expression (*in voce*). Odo rejected the novel, incipient nominalism he found among those who preferred the authority of Aristotle and Porphyry[24] to that of Boethius and Plato.

Although Odo complains of those who now followed Aristotle and Porphyry in the increasingly intense debate over the status of universals, it should be noted that the likely sources he has in mind, namely Aristotle's *Categories* and *On Interpretation*, and Porphyry's *Isagoge*, had been available in some form to the Latin world for centuries, even if not read widely. What was new was the appearance of scholars willing to consider the possibility that the widely accepted Platonized view of universals was mistaken. This debate, despite its seemingly abstract and arcane nature, would grow in importance once it entered the universities in the thirteenth and fourteenth centuries. During Odo's career its implications were not yet fully understood, nor was it a purely philosophical debate. The nature of universals emerged as a serious concern primarily because of its perceived theological implications, resulting not infrequently in attacks on philosophy itself for placing in doubt established doctrine.[25] Thus one of the early proponents of nominalism, Roscelin of Compiegne, was condemned at the Council of Soissons in 1092 because frightened churchmen believed that his view on the nature of universals threatened the dogma of the Trinity.[26] If universals do not actually exist but are only convenient terms we use to describe resemblances among real individuals then, they concluded, Roscelin must be guilty of denying that the divine nature — which the three persons Father, Son, and Holy Spirit have in common — actually exists in reality. Although Roscelin did recant, both Anselm of Canterbury and Ivo of Chartres upbraid him for having returned to his errors after the council. Anselm complains that Roscelin only abjured his errors at Soissons because he feared that he would otherwise have been killed by the townspeople. This would indicate that the controversy had perhaps moved beyond the rarified air of the schools and monasteries to a more public venue.[27] Furthermore, as we will show later, Odo's own treatise *On Original Sin* suggests that for him nominalism threatened to undermine the "orthodox" teaching on the nature of the soul and its origins. His interest in original sin and its transmission appears, then, to reflect the concerns of the debate over universals.

Quite apart from its philosophical and theological impact, this debate over the nature of universals had economic consequences. New doctrines attracted students and supported the emergence of many schools in the late eleventh and early twelfth centuries. For Odo and the chapter at Notre Dame, adherence to the "doctrine of the ancients" could have a grave economic impact. Raimbert, master of the school at nearby Lille, had adopted the new philosophical ideas and was drawing students away from Tournai. Although Herman disapproved of his teaching, he notes that many other students were drawn to his lectures rather than Odo's not simply by human curiosity but also by Raimbert's flashy eloquence. Since Odo contradicted Raimbert on universals and Raimbert publicly declared that his teaching on the nature of universals was superior to Odo's, their students were left confused. One of these was a clerk named Gualbert, who would later become a monk of St. Martin of Tournai before ascending to the episcopacy. When he was unable to resolve the difficult issues involved in the debate over universals, Gualbert sought to find the true doctrine by appealing to a well-known oracle, a deaf mute who resided at Tournai. Using sign language, he asked the oracle which master ought to be believed: Odo or Raimbert? Drawing his hand across his left palm in the manner of one drawing in the sand, and pointing his finger toward Tournai, the oracle indicated that Odo's doctrine was correct. Pointing in the direction of Lille, the oracle blew through his hand with his mouth, in order to indicate that Raimbert's teaching was just a lot of hot air. Herman evidently repeats this story, not in order to recommend oracles, but simply to reveal that those scholars who base their doctrine on Aristotle or Porphyry rather than Boethius and the ancients ought to be "blown away" and ignored,[28] as Anselm of Canterbury had recommended also.[29]

Although Odo's teaching continued to attract students to Tournai, it was also the discipline he imposed among his students that recommended the cathedral school. It was both for this school discipline (or "religion") and for his knowledge that Odo was praised. His students were sober and attentive. They did not dare to laugh,[30] or even to move their eyes to the right or to the left. The school was not disrupted by new styles in clothing or hair, nor by visits by women. Laymen were not allowed to enter the cloister during the hour when Odo instructed his disciples. Odo eliminated the customary practice of hearing law cases in the cloister, forbidding entrance even to Everard, the powerful castellan of the city. A visitor to the school "would see master Odo at one moment walking with his disciples and teaching, according to the custom of the Peripatetics, at another sitting like the Stoics and solving diverse questions, and then at the hour of vespers and even into the dead of night disputing before the doors of the church."[31] For Herman, one could hardly find more "religion" in the strict monastic observance at Cluny than in Odo's philosophical discipline at the cathedral school.

Since the students were discussing questions of natural science or philosophy, Odo's school discipline may seem to have had little religious content. Still, Odo's students were clerks and they did participate in the divine office at the church of Notre Dame. Moreover, one can not draw a line too sharply at this time between theology, philosophy, and natural science. Even discussions of astronomy could arise from the religious need to calculate properly the dates for religious festivals based upon the lunar calendar. But the titles of Odo's early works, works no longer extant, suggest what we might call a secular orientation: *The Sophist*, which instructed one how to avoid being led astray by errors of logic; the *Book of Consequences* (*Liber complexionum*), a second treatise on dialectic; and *On Substance and Being* (*De re et ente*), "in which he resolved [the question] whether a substance (*res*) and being (*ens*) are one and the same."[32] While some of his contemporaries might have viewed Odo's school as designed to instruct students in the liberal arts rather than in the spiritual discipline of the monastery, his biographer regards it as essentially "religious" for the simple reason that Odo excluded laymen from the cloister at the time of his lectures.[33] His teaching was only for the initiate, and not for the crowd, and it unveiled mysteries of reason which those outside the school could not be expected to appreciate.

Odo's Conversion and Monastic Foundation

Herman's description of the "religious" character of the school, however, helps to prepare his reader for the sudden conversion that Odo experienced five years after his arrival at the cathedral school — a conversion that led him to abandon the school for the rigors of the eremitic life.[34] This dramatic conversion was precipitated by an encounter with Augustine's writings. Odo had purchased a copy of Augustine's *On Free Will* (*De libero arbitrio*) "for the sole purpose of increasing his library" and then "threw the book into a chest with his other books since, still occupied with worldly wisdom, he delighted more in reading Plato than Augustine."[35] Only several months later, when Odo was examining the doctrine of free will in the fourth book of Boethius's *Consolation of Philosophy*, did he remember that he had purchased a work by Augustine whose title also promised a discussion on free will. The third book of Augustine's *On Free Will*, which addresses the paradox that God necessarily foreknows those actions we will to do freely, forcefully struck Odo.[36] Perhaps as important as Augustine's argument was his evocative description of the soul's condition. Herman explains:

> [Odo] began to read from the third book, in which the forementioned doctor [Augustine] compares sinful souls to a slave struck down from his earlier dignity for his crimes, and consigned to the sewer of this world, which souls have lost celestial glory for their crimes, adorning this world which is like a fetid sewer as long as they live in it. When master Odardus[37] [Odo] read this passage to his disciples, he was inwardly gripped with a certain heartache and, drawing a deep breath, he said: "Alas, how heavily this passage weighs upon us! Truly this seems so clearly to apply as if it were written just for us! We only adorn this fetid world a little with our knowledge, but we will be unworthy of celestial glory after death, because we do not serve God nor apply our knowledge in his service, but rather we abuse it in worldly vanity for earthly praise." After he said this, he rose up, entirely bathed in tears, and entered the church. Suddenly the whole school was disturbed; even the canons gathered there were struck by a special admiration.[38]

After this, Odo was absent from the school for some time. He began to frequent the church, bringing alms he had collected for the poor, and imposed a severe penitential discipline upon himself. He fasted until his appearance was entirely transformed. When he finally returned to the school, he was so lean and gaunt that his students hardly recognized him. Quickly the word spread that Odo would renounce the world and undertake the religious life. Five of his disciples resolved to follow him: Rodulf, Willelm, Gerbert, and Lanfred. The fifth and unnamed companion, Herman remarks, abandoned the monastic life, forsook his vows, and died as a result.

Abbots from nearby monasteries and communities of canons regular came to Tournai in order to invite Odo and his disciples to join them, with the expectation that Odo's reputation would add prestige to their foundations. Initially, Odo's companions were attracted to the community of canons at Mont-Saint-Éloi, near Arras, which had been reformed in 1068. Perhaps reflecting a common monastic criticism of the customs followed by canons regular, Herman remarks that Odo and his companions initially preferred "to assume the order of canons rather than monks, because they found the rites of the canons in ecclesiastical offices and [their customs pertaining to] food and clothing more tolerable than the monk's."[39] Although in principle canons were bound also to seek apostolic perfection, the *Institutio canonicorum*, promulgated in the Carolingian period, relaxed considerably the obligations of canons with respect to matters of diet, clothing, and private property, providing concessions that monks did not enjoy. Thus they were not prohibited from wearing linen, eating meat, or retaining their private possessions.

Despite Odo's intention to leave the world for the religious life, he and his companions suffered a good deal of uncertainty when trying to decide where to go and what to do. This uncertainty must have been magnified by the increasing variety of options available to them at that time. Among others, they could approach a traditional Benedictine community following the Rule of St. Benedict; they could enter a community of canons regular following (more or less) an Augustinian rule; or they could strike out in search of a perfect eremitic life based on the precepts of the desert fathers, as others had in France or as the disciples of St. Romuald had in Italy at Pomposa, Fonte Avellana, and elsewhere.[40]

While each of these options in the religious life might be viewed as good, they were not equally good. Although the number of candidates entering traditional Benedictine monasteries continued to increase in the period 1050–1150, there was nevertheless a growing perception that the religious path pursued by Benedictine monasticism was somewhat less secure or less meritorious than had been assumed previously. This perception was not grounded in the obvious: namely, that some monasteries were badly in need of reform and had failed to live up to the standards St. Benedict had established. Rather, it seems to have been based in the awareness that although the Black monks had taken vows of poverty, nevertheless the development of Benedictine monasticism in the Carolingian age relied on a definition of poverty and apostolic perfection that was no longer satisfying to large numbers in pursuit of the ideal religious life.[41]

The source of this dissatisfaction can be traced to the ninth-century monastic reformer Benedict of Aniane and the council of Aix-la-Chapelle (A.D. 817). These had attempted to introduce greater uniformity of practice to Benedictine houses. Since by this time more and more monks were also priests, their efforts naturally focused on the performance of a greatly expanded liturgy. While this liturgical cycle may have been received by monk-priests as the proper end for their activity, it reduced, as a consequence, the time (and energy) available for manual labor. The virtual disappearance of manual labor from the Benedictine regimen not only effected the transformation of the monastic ideal, but resulted too in a monastic culture that relied more and more on fixed and stable revenues derived from ecclesiastical tithes, donations, and landed wealth. This wealth was necessary to support the expansion of a liturgy for which, soon, even the monastic day would appear to be too short; which was celebrated with great pomp, splendor, and increasingly elaborate musical settings; and which employed expensive vestments, liturgical instruments, and altar pieces. Although the monks were dedicated to individual poverty, the fixed properties and wealth necessary to endow this sort of activity placed them (or the leaders of their communities) among the ranks of the great and powerful lords of feudal society.

One can explain the rapid growth of other options in religious life during the eleventh and twelfth centuries as a response to this situation. Across Europe individuals and small communities found it impossible to reconcile the position of monastic officials as feudal lords with the positive model of Christ's poor. The poverty, humility, and sense of community they understood to be present among the apostles they saw only very imperfectly realized by the Black monks. As a result, those looking for an alternative raised up once again the twin virtues of manual labor and apostolic poverty. The expanding eremitic movement, which viewed the religious life of the hermit as one that restored a proper emphasis to manual labor and poverty, insisted on a return to a simpler life, one without rich vestments, splendid buildings, and a highly embellished liturgy.[42] Implicitly criticizing the wealth of Benedictine institutions that had become examples of a Church whose wealth and splendor dazzled the senses, they sought to become once again poor and humble servants of the Lord, laborers in the fields or towns of Christendom, carrying with them not the paradigm of Christ in glory but that of Christ crucified.[43]

The renewed appeal of apostolic poverty and manual labor as symbols not only of religious austerity and dedication but also of the perfection of the primitive Christian community need not suggest that the eremitic movement rejected the Benedictine ideal, especially at a time when the great foundation of Cluny was working, with some success, on improving the customs of monks throughout much of Europe. Relations between eremitic communities or individual hermits and Benedictine houses may be described as generally cordial. Oftentimes individual hermits or communities of hermits passed through stages that involved, at least for a time, the acceptance of Benedictine customs.[44] Nevertheless, as Benedict himself acknowledged, his Rule for monks was intended only as a *beginning* for those striving to ascend the ladder of perfection. The alternative forged by the eremitic movement was understood by many hermits to exist for those intent on climbing higher.

The desire, not necessarily to condemn and repudiate Benedictine monasticism but to rise above it on the ladder of perfection, also inspired a movement to reform the life of canons regular. Some of the same concerns expressed by eremitic reformers will be found among those seeking to reform clerical life and help to explain the growing popularity of this path as a religious alternative. By the pontificate of Urban II at the end of the eleventh century many clergy living in collegiate or cathedral churches had adopted the Rule of St. Augustine, emphasizing not only the obligation of celibacy but equally a requirement for a common life that eschewed in principle private property.[45] Reform among canons regular, then, also sought to revive what was perceived to be the salient character of the apostolic community: an emphasis on poverty and communal responsibility each for the other.[46]

This need for reform among the regular clergy can in one sense be traced back as well to the religious reforms at the council of Aix-la-Chapelle. The council sought to clarify the juridical distinction between canons and monks and established a rule or customary for canons (the *Institutio canonicorum*) influenced by the ideals of Jerome, Augustine, and the influential Carolingian Bishop, Chrodegang of Metz. This rule acknowledged that canons too have a vocation to seek evangelical perfection, but relaxed the standards for canons regarding dress, diet, and the principle of poverty. Again, the rule allowed canons the use and possession of private property, despite Augustine's advice to the contrary; permitted them a diet that did not exclude meat (which Benedict's Rule forbade to monks who were not old or infirm); and provided for clothes of finer materials (e.g., linen) than monks enjoyed. While many of the canons who followed the guidelines established at Aix-la-Chapelle led exemplary lives, resided in a community of clerks (with a common dormitory and refectory), and performed their religious duties scrupulously, others had fallen away, abandoned the model of communal living, neglected the needs of their church, and scandalized the faithful by ignoring the obligation of priestly celibacy.

In response, reformers who criticized the life of canons regular emphasized again the ideals of the apostolic community. The movement received impetus and inspiration not only from members of the ecclesiastical hierarchy, but equally from leaders of the eremitic movement like Romuald of Ravenna. These reformers did not fail to point out the contradiction between the ideals espoused by Augustine and the rather more relaxed rule established at Aix-la-Chapelle.[47] They also emphasized the positive value of manual labor as a religious ideal. As a result, some communities of canons regular drew closer to the eremitic model, while retaining a more pastoral orientation than one would expect to find among hermits.[48]

Despite reform efforts throughout the entire Church and its religious communities, however, a perception remained, evidently shared by a growing number of individuals, that Benedictine monasticism did not (or, perhaps, could not) perfectly realize the ideals of the apostolic life; that even in its reformed state it failed to imitate satisfactorily the evangelical ideal of poverty; and, that it had too long neglected the positive value of manual labor. This perception helps to explain what historians have called a "crisis" for Benedictine monasticism. This "crisis" cannot be quantifiably measured. It apparently did not result in a decline in the number of entrants to the monasteries, nor did it result in a decline in donations to monastic institutions. But it did contribute to the remarkable growth of alternative forms of religious life in the eleventh and twelfth centuries already described.[49] As a result, it is understandable that Odo and his companions would have been uncertain and perhaps confused as they sought to formalize their decision to undertake a religious life. Which path, they wondered, is best?

Faced with this proliferation of options, it may have seemed providential to Herman that the people of Tournai and its bishop, Rabod II, made the decision for Odo and his companions. Following the end of the epidemic described earlier, everyone in Tournai wanted to restore the little church of St. Martin and install a community of monks there.[50] This was no easy matter, however. The church was in ruins and its alienated lands were held as benefices by powerful noble families. Fastred, advocate for the city of Tournai, complained that he could persuade no monks from neighboring provinces to enter St. Martin's because "he had found none who wished to enter into such great poverty."[51] The church of St. Martin, then, was hardly an attractive site for Odo and his companions.

When the bishop, following the entreaties of the townspeople, offered Odo and his followers St. Martin's, their reaction was perhaps predictable. Odo was afraid that they would be unable to survive, let alone prosper, at a place that had been largely destroyed. But Rabod II persuaded him that it is necessary to suffer many hardships in order to enter the kingdom of God (Acts 14:22). Odo and his companions agreed to accept St. Martin's as the site for their religious community, under these conditions: that the church should be conferred on them by episcopal privilege, and be free from every exaction. While the bishop was willing to accept these conditions, the canons of the cathedral of Notre Dame were not. They were afraid that such an arrangement would diminish their prestige in the province, not to mention their revenues. Rabod II overcame these objections only by reminding the canons of the obedience they owed him and by agreeing that he would not bestow on St. Martin's anything from their parishes without their consent.[52] Once these conditions were met, Odo and his companions received the habit of canons regular at St. Martin's in May, 1092.

The concerns expressed by the canons at the church of Notre Dame were not without justification. During its first year pious laypeople in the city gathered alms for the new community and erected a wooden building next to the church. The number of Odo's disciples grew from five to eighteen, despite its poverty.[53] Nevertheless, this growth did not bring wealth to St. Martin's. Indeed, Odo consciously embraced a strict definition of evangelical poverty as a model and guide for his community.[54] But one might feel — as the canons of Notre Dame must have — that material and human resources that would otherwise have come to enrich their church were being diverted to support this new community. One of the first confrontations Odo had with the canons of Notre Dame involved the efforts of a young clerk, Alufus, to join them. His father Siger, the cantor (*precentor*) at Notre Dame, was furious that his son had joined the new community. Siger burst into St. Martin's and seized the boy by the hair, violently dragging him back to Notre Dame. The next day, however, Alufus returned to St. Martin's, and again his father dragged him back. This occurred so many times that Odo consulted the abbot of Anchin, Haimeric, and asked him what he should do. Although it was itself a recent foundation, Anchin had already achieved a reputation for rigor and sanctity. Haimeric answered:

> Truly, good master, what is happening with this boy will happen often with your other brothers unless you become monks. For you live near a city, and your younger brothers may easily be influenced by their friends, secular clerks, to return to the world, because you wear one and the same habit. If, however, you were monks, then they would try to return none of yours to the world because, since the habit of monks is black, and that of clerks white, clerks regard the habit of monks with such great horror that one whom they see has become a monk they will never again have as a friend. Consider too that the life of clerks is softer and more relaxed, even of those living according to a rule, inasmuch as they are clothed in linen, frequently eat meat, and only read nine lessons on feast days. . . . I advise you and your clerks, then, to seek the stricter rather than the more relaxed order.[55]

The following day, Odo and twelve members of the community put aside their clerical vestments and were clothed with a monastic habit. Those who had sung matins and prime as canons thenceforth would sing the hours of the divine office as monks, chanting twelve lessons on feast days, for example, rather than nine. Haimeric's advice evidently solved Odo's problem: when Siger saw that his son had become a monk, he did not try to recover him for the community at Notre Dame. Later, Siger himself and his brother Herman became monks at St. Martin's, establishing a precedent that others would follow. Odo received men, women, and children of the region from every social class. Among them were Walter (Gualterius) and Radulf of Osmunt;[56] Fastred (the advocate of Tournai), his wife Ida, and her daughter-in-law, Richel; and, Radulf and Mainsend, Herman's parents, with their four sons.[57] Radulf's example was persuasive, and on account of his conversion several important citizens of Tournai became monks under Odo. Herman mentions Henry, a very wealthy man, his wife Bertha, and their three children, and adds that "After Henry, you saw youths and virgins, old and young, coming in great numbers from all over the province, abandoning the world, and coming to conversion."[58]

The reception of women and whole families is not unique to St. Martin's, but remains unusual nevertheless.[59] It is a testimony to the growing spiritual fervor that new experiments in religious life generated at this time among the laity. What is surprising is the number of women who must have approached St. Martin's — so many that Odo was compelled to construct two separate monasteries for them. In the first, he established some sixty women and set his sister, Eremburg, over them; in the second, he established an equal number of women (*conversas*) under a second mistress (*magistra*).[60]

Apostolic Poverty and the Appeal of the "Desert"

Odo and his early disciples insisted on a much stricter application of the principle of apostolic poverty than was observed at many other communities. This ideal of poverty did not forbid the receipt of gifts or donations; it did mean that the gifts and donations Odo received were not used to enrich the community itself, but were quickly disbursed in charitable operations. Odo wanted no silver chalice, cross, or tapestry to ornament his church, "nor did he wish to make golden crosses, but disbursed all the money which was brought to him to the poor and oppressed."[61] Odo thought of himself as a dispensor or administrator of the wealth of the church, and not its lord or possessor.

In the early years of this new foundation, however, Odo did reject an entire category of income he feared would diminish the spiritual integrity of his new experiment: ecclesiastical revenues and altars. While this decision threatened to undermine the community's financial security, it nevertheless inspired others to join it and participate in Odo's experiment. This is made quite explicit in the vita of the prior Gonhardus, who was received by Odo. Gonhardus brought with him three other canons from St. Mary of Tournai. All accepted the monk's habit because they were inspired by Odo's rejection of ecclesiastical benefices.[62] Fifty years later Herman remarks, perhaps unhappily, that "If he [Odo] had wished to receive the altars which they [those entering the community] held then, perhaps today our church would be richer; but because he proposed to receive neither altars nor churches nor revenues, but to live only from the labor of their hands, from the cultivation of fields and the raising of flocks, he wanted nothing to do with the ecclesiastical tithes which they held, saying that such things belonged only to clerks and ought not be possessed by monks."[63] Rather than live off the tithes and revenues generated from ecclesiastical properties held by those entering his community, Odo insisted that the monks work in the fields. This emphasis on manual labor is a common element in the eremitic reform movement of the late eleventh and early twelfth century, and supports Dereine's depiction of Odo as a "hermit by desire."[64] In Odo's community, while his monks worked the fields, the women were occupied with spinning flax and weaving.[65]

This ideal form of apostolic poverty did not long survive a catastrophic famine in the region in the winter of 1095. The famine severely tested the community, as I have shown elsewhere.[66] The future of the monastery was so tenuous that the management of its income and properties was removed from Odo's hands and given to Radulf, while Odo continued to govern only its spiritual life.[67] Radulf radically revised the community's understanding of religious poverty. Recognizing the danger the famine presented to the foundation, Radulf insisted that it could not survive without more extensive holdings. He persuaded his brother, Theodoric, to donate gold, silver, and lands to the monastery. Radulf purchased draft animals, constructed new buildings in which to house them, and worked to improve the agricultural yield from the land the monks worked. Most important, however, he insisted that they could no longer afford to reject tithes, altars, and ecclesiastical revenues new entrants to the community brought with them. Odo acquiesced, and thenceforth received a large number of canons whose income helped the community to survive. Albert D'Haenens has calculated that in roughly the period from Odo's abbacy to Herman's (about fifty years), St. Martin of Tournai acquired thirty-seven altars, with an annual income approaching 220 pounds.[68]

It may not be mere coincidence that about this same time, in September 1095 (six months after the community had accepted the monastic habit from abbot Haimeric of Anchin), Odo and his monks sought to abandon St. Martin's in search of a better site, a "desert" where they would not be distracted by the proximity of a town and its culture. The attractions of life in the town had, Herman admits, weakened the community. One night after matins the monks put their library[69] in a cart and resolved to follow Odo out of the province as quickly as possible. When the citizens of Tournai discovered the monks' absence and learned that they were en route to Noyon in order to petition the bishop, Rabod II, for permission to leave the province, they quickly sent a message to the bishop. The townspeople threatened that if the bishop ever hoped to return to Tournai he had better refuse the monks' request.

The bishop was easily persuaded. He sent a troop of knights to meet the monks on the road and bring them to Noyon on horseback. The monks, constrained by humility, refused to ride and continued on foot to Noyon. There the bishop reminded the monks that they were "constrained by the bonds of obedience"[70] and commanded them to return to Tournai. Once the monks had returned to Tournai, the citizens asked the bishop to restore ancient holdings of St. Martin's that had come into his hands when the monastery had been ruined in the ninth century but were enjoyed by the advocate of Tournai and others as a benefice. The bishop did manage to restore some lands to St. Martin's without feudal obligation (*libera*).[71]

This anecdote indicates the interest that the people of Tournai had in the community. Not only did Odo's presence add to the prestige of the area, but its economy also likely benefited from St. Martin's. Perhaps Odo made the restoration of these lands a condition for the voluntary return of the monks, just as earlier he had insisted on certain episcopal privileges before he agreed to establish his disciples there. Or perhaps it was the bishop (as well as certain members of the community at St. Martin's) who urged Odo to modify his commitment to apostolic poverty and to accept these posses- sions for the foundation's stability and growth, for soon after the monks returned to Tournai the bishop prevailed on them to control their desire to imitate the desert fathers and to accept the rule followed at Cluny. St. Martin's received monks from Anchin for instruction in the customs of Cluny,[72] among whom it was clearly understood that Cluny was willing to accept lands and revenues as monastic possessions for the benefit of the foundation itself. It also would receive daughter houses or priories, extend- ing the reach of the community beyond Tournai itself. One early example is the addition of the community of Odomez, which Lambert, Bishop of (newly independent) Arras, placed under the control of St. Martin of Tournai.[73]

From this time on the community made a concerted effort to recover its ancient possessions. This required not only an effort to persuade those who held these possessions to donate them to the monastery, but also an effort simply to identify those possessions. During the devastating inva- sions of the ninth century, many monastic charters and documents had been lost. Herman himself traveled to an abbey in Ferrières, outside Paris, when he learned that some of these lost documents could be found in its library.[74] In a nearby church in the village of Souppes sur Loing, Herman claims he saw an old and rotting codex, entitled *Liber Sancti Martini Tornacensis cenobii*, which identified that very village, and certain mills in the area, as the property of St. Martin of Tournai. These possessions were now in the hands of a powerful knight and Herman was unable to recover them.

Not all the community's possessions, though, were so distant from Tournai itself. Some, as already mentioned, belonged to the advocate of Tournai and were recovered by the monastery when Odo and his disciples returned there. Others, including relics of Martin of Tournai himself, were suspected of having fallen into the hands of the canons of the church of Notre Dame.[75] These disputed possessions became the subject of protracted litigation and led to violent confrontations between the two communities. The canons of Notre Dame complained to Pope Paschal II that St. Martin of Tournai did not deserve abbatial status but should be merely a chapel under their jurisdiction. They repudiated the monks' claim that their church unjustly held possessions belonging to St. Martin, and the canons petitioned the Pope to rescind a privilege he had granted to the monks to bury those who wished to be buried at the monastery.[76]

The dispute between these two communities threatened to plunge the whole region into civil war, for it involved not only the monks and canons but also their powerful relations. For example, Herman alleges that the clerks of Tournai hired mercenaries to attack the community of St. Martin and set fire to its buildings. When these even beat one of the monks, Gerulf, who had been a renowned knight prior to his conversion, Gerulf's powerful friends outside the monastery attacked the clerks of Tournai and slew eighteen of them.[77]

Despite papal support for the monks, it was laypeople in Tournai who arranged a compromise: the monks would agree to tithe one tenth to the church of Notre Dame, and the canons would not dispute their right to offer burial.[78] It appears, then, that the canons at Notre Dame had good reason to fear the precedent the bishop, Rabod II, had established when he granted certain episcopal privileges and exemptions to Odo and his community. As time passed, they competed more and more closely not only for new members, but also for revenues, income, and resources. The competition did not lead to the decline of Odo's monastic community, however. By the end of the thirteenth century the monastery of St. Martin of Tournai had become one of the truly great Benedictine houses in western Europe.[79]

Bishop of Cambrai

After more than a decade as abbot of St. Martin of Tournai, Odo was elevated to the bishopric of Cambrai and consecrated by Archbishop Manasses of Reims on 2 July 1105. Herman may reflect the common view of the monks at St. Martin's when he laments that on that day "the crown suddenly fell from our head and joy left our heart."[80]

Cambrai was a not very large town just south of Tournai. But the diocese in which the bishop of Cambrai exercised his spiritual authority was vast, and included five archdiaconates: Cambrai, Hainaut, Valenciennes, Brabant, and Anvers.[81] For most of the eleventh century, the bishops of Cambrai were vassals of the emperor who exercised de facto if not de jure the seigneurial rights of feudal lords. Episcopal power in Cambrai, however, began to erode during the last decade of the eleventh century, as evidenced by the successful efforts of the ancient diocese of Arras to separate from Cambrai, to which it had been attached since the late sixth century.[82] The power of the bishop was also challenged by the citizens of Cambrai, who had created a revolutionary commune there in 1077 in order to secure certain rights. On more than one occasion over the next thirty years the people of Cambrai rose in armed insurrection, until the emperor intervened energetically in 1106 on behalf of the rights of the episcopacy.[83]

While the monks may have grieved when they learned that Odo would depart for Cambrai, Odo may not himself have been very pleased to enter that long-troubled see. Certainly many of the citizens of Cambrai were unhappy with his election. For more than ten years Cambrai had been involved in an unresolved dispute between the pope and the emperor over the investiture of its prelate.[84] Bishop Walcher (or Gaucher/Galcher) had been invested by the emperor, Henry IV, in 1093. At Clermont, however, in 1095 Pope Urban II had him deposed as a simoniac. Manasses of Soissons was elected to the now "vacant" bishopric, but Walcher refused to give up his episcopal throne. After years of strife, Pope Paschal II was unable to install Manasses and was compelled to transfer him to Soissons.[85] In this contested see, lay lords took advantage of the conflict in order to expand their own power and control, at the expense of the bishopric.

But Paschal II did not abandon Cambrai. He instructed Archbishop Manasses of Reims to hold a council, at which Odo of Tournai was elected as the reform candidate. Odo also was unable to seat Walcher and only eight days later he returned to St. Martin's. For the next year Odo exercised episcopal authority from Tournai, at least to the extent that he was able. In 1106 the emperor ceded Cambrai to Robert II, count of Flanders. Although the Emperor, Henry V, was accompanied by Walcher, Robert installed Odo in the episcopal see.[86] Despite Henry's support, Walcher was forced to renounce his claim upon Cambrai at the peace of Aix-la-Chapelle (December 1107), and retire to a monastery.

As bishop, Odo attended a council at Troyes in February 1107[87] and was active in establishing new monastic foundations in the region.[88] But the conflict involving Count Robert II of Flanders, Emperor Henry V, and the pope, would again force him to flee Cambrai. In the prologue to his work, *De blasphemia in Spiritum Sanctum*, Odo explains that when he later refused to accept ring and staff, the symbols of episcopal authority, from the hand of the emperor he was forced into exile.[89] He retired to the monastery of Anchin[90] where several years later he died,[91] on 19 June[92] 1113 (the feast day of the Bl. Odo of Cambrai).[93]

Works of Odo of Tournai

As indicated earlier, Odo's lost early works, *The Sophist*, the *Book of Consequences* or *Conclusions* (*Liber complexionum*), and *On Substance and Being* (*De re et ente*), were probably written while he was still at the cathedral school of Notre Dame. Although Herman briefly describes these writings,[94] a mortuary roll from Anchin identifies all Odo's works except these as present in the monastic library.[95] Since Odo died at Anchin and since St. Martin's always had a very close relationship with this monastery, it seems peculiar that these works should be missing unless Odo had moved beyond his philosophical works written before his monastic conversion. Also from this period is a youthful poem on the Trojan War, *De bello troianae*, sometimes attributed to Odo, which Godfrey of Reims praised in his *Dream of Odo of Orléans* (*Somnium de Odone Aurelianensi*).[96] There is some question, however, whether Godfrey's work is addressed to Odo of Cambrai or Odo of Meung.[97] This poem has disappeared,[98] although it may still have been available in Paris in the eighteenth century.[99] In addition to *De bello troianae* several other works of doubtful authenticity, no longer extant, are sometimes attributed to Odo of Tournai. These include a *Book of Conferences* (*Liber collationum*), *Discussions upon the Psalter* (*Distinctiones super psalterium*), an *Introduction to Theology*, a *Book of Parables* and a *Homily on the Passion* (these two may be the work of Odo of Canterbury), and an *Exposition on the Number Three*.[100]

Once Odo assumed the responsibilities first of abbot and then of bishop, he presented a large number of beautifully crafted sermons to his community. It was Odo's sermon on the Incarnation that led Herman of Tournai, his biographer, to compose a work of his own on that subject, drawing both from Odo's sermon and Anselm of Canterbury's *Cur Deus*

Homo.[101] Regrettably, only one of Odo's sermons has survived, entitled "Homo quidem erat dives qui habebat villicum." This sermon on the text of Luke 16: 1 is found in two versions — one shorter and one longer — in J.P. Migne's *Patrologia cursus completus, Series Latina*, vol. 160: 1121–1128 and 1131–1150.[102]

Most of Odo's remaining works can be found in this same volume in Migne's *Patrologia*. These include his *Exposition on the Canon of the Mass* (*Expositio in canonem missae*), a detailed explanation of the mass and its symbolism written during Odo's episcopate that represents a significant contribution to the development of liturgical theology in the Middle Ages.[103] During his exile at the monastery of Anchin, Odo wrote *On Blasphemy Against the Holy Spirit* (*De Blasphemia in Spiritum Sanctum*)[104] in an effort to reconcile seemingly discordant opinions found in the synoptic Gospels and John over forgiveness and the character of unforgiveable sin. This same interest in overcoming opposition among the gospel texts, and in establishing a rule of interpretation, is present in Odo's *On the Canons of the Gospels* (*De Canonibus Evangeliorum*).[105] The works included in this volume, however, represent his principal work:[106] *On Original Sin* (*De peccato originali*),[107] and his *Disputation with the Jew, Leo, concerning the advent of Christ, the Son of God* (*Disputatio contra Judaeum Leonem nomine de adventu Christi filii Dei*).[108] Both these works will receive special attention below.

In addition to letters from Odo's episcopacy confirming charters and privileges for churches in his diocese[109] we also have a work in verse attributed to Odo of Tournai that is included within the literary corpus of Hildebert of Lavardin, entitled *On the Works of the Six Days* [*of Creation*] (*De operibus sex dierum*).[110] This is a long poetic dilation on Genesis 1–2. Besides Odo's original compositions, however, we also possess manuscripts copied during his abbacy in the scriptorium, for example Bibliothèque nationale lat. 2195, a copy of the Psalter. Odo developed a truly exceptional monastic library and scriptorium at St. Martin of Tournai.[111] His biographer insists that the abbey library was the most impressive in the entire region and that other communities regularly sent their texts to St. Martin of Tournai for correction.[112]

On Original Sin

Odo's most important work is his *On Original Sin* (*De peccato originali*). This treatise, which Odo claims he wrote only after much prodding from the monks in his community, is both a theological *excursus* on the character of that sin all inherit from Adam, and a philosophical investigation of the manner in which the sin of an individual, Adam, can be transmitted to the species, humanity. It raises a number of questions which, ultimately, Odo is unable to resolve. This is not so much Odo's failure, however, as it is a reflection of the real difficulties these questions conceal, difficulties that plagued the fathers as well as the medieval doctors of the Church.

Although there were early disagreements over the right understanding of original sin and its consequences, a consensus gradually emerged in the western Church following the debates between St. Augustine and the followers of Pelagius early in the fifth century. Pelagius's disciple Celestius was condemned for the view that Adam's sin affected only Adam, not the entire human race. Other Pelagians (or semi-Pelagians) reasonably inferred that "If sin is natural, it is not voluntary; if it is voluntary, it is not inborn. These two definitions are as mutually contrary as are necessity and [free] will."[113] Since the Pelagians insisted on the voluntary character of sin, it seemed to them impossible that one might be born with sin. Augustine, on the other hand, affirms that original sin is both voluntary and free for Adam, while it is natural and necessary in us. In part this view stems from Augustine's efforts to safeguard the traditional practice of infant baptism in the Church, which can be defended if there is some inherited sin of which infants must be cleansed. In part it stems from Augustine's reading of one Vulgate version of Romans 5: 12, which identifies Adam as the one in whom all have sinned and through whom sin and death have entered the world.[114] Because all humanity has participated in the sin of the first man, Augustine avers, all mankind constitutes now a *massa perditionis* or a *massa damnata*,[115] a single lump of sin,[116] a lump of filth.[117]

While Augustine insists that every person participates in and inherits Adam's sin and its consequences, he is not very clear about precisely how this sin is transmitted to subsequent generations or to the whole of human nature. When asked to explain the origin of the soul and the transmission of original sin, Augustine eliminates the views of the Pythagoreans and the Origenists, who claim that the soul fell from heaven and entered a body as a punishment for previous sins.[118] He refutes also the Stoics, Manichaeans, and Priscillianists, who argue that the soul is an emanation from the divine substance. Finally, Augustine attacks Tertullian's view that the individual soul is produced from a material seed or root-stock (*tradux*) of the parent. But he himself is unable to decide between two remaining options: creationism and spiritual traducianism.[119] Creationism, a view Augustine attributes to Jerome,[120] maintains that God creates ex nihilo each new individual soul and infuses it in the body generated from sexual intercourse. This infusion occurs either at the moment of conception or forty days later in the womb. Spiritual traducianism maintains that the individual soul is generated from a parent soul or spiritual principle: "as light is kindled from light and from it a second flame comes into existence without loss to the first, so a soul comes into existence in a child from the soul of the parent, or is transferred to the child."[121] Both positions, Augustine maintains, can be defended by an appeal to the canonical Scriptures.

In a letter addressed to Jerome, Augustine reveals his uncertainty, but seems to follow Jerome's preference for the creationist solution.[122] Still, elsewhere he confesses that so long as we are agreed that all suffer from original sin and require God's grace in order to be freed from this sin and its consequences, the question of the origin of the soul and the transmission of original sin can remain undecided without danger. Augustine remarks in a sort of parable that, "Someone once fell into a well where the water was of such depth that it supported him so that he did not drown, but not so deep as to choke him so that he could not speak. A bystander came over when he saw him and asked sympathetically: 'How did you fall in?' He answered: 'Please find some way of getting me out and never mind how I fell in.'"[123] His conclusion is that it is not as important to know how we fell into the well of sin as it is to find the way out.

Odo's contemporaries confirmed the repudiation of an emanationist doctrine of the soul's origin, compelled to do so again, perhaps, by a new interest in the work of Macrobius.[124] But most Christian thinkers, at least until the thirteenth century, reflected Augustine's uncertainty when reviewing the creationist and traducianist alternatives. Cassiodorus,[125] Gregory the Great, Isidore of Seville, Prudentius,[126] Rabanus Maurus,[127] Agobard of Lyon,[128] and others, generally preferred the creationist solution, but often hesitated to condemn traducianism altogether.[129] In the eleventh century, Odorannus of Sens defended creationism, after reviewing the work of Gregory, Prudentius, and Isidore.[130] He was joined by Werner of St. Blaise.[131] In the twelfth century, Hugh de Ribemont took up the defense of creationism.[132] Although in the twelfth and thirteenth centuries some continued to hesitate between traducianism and creationism,[133] traducianism began to appear not only as a less probable solution but also as false, impious, and, ultimately, heretical. This change appeared in Peter Lombard,[134] Robert Pullen,[135] Albertus Magnus,[136] Thomas Aquinas,[137] and others. Finally, the Fifth Lateran Council, under Pope Leo X, defined as

Catholic doctrine that souls created from nothing are infused in each new body.[138]

It is especially in the eleventh and twelfth centuries that one finds new interest expressed in the origin of the soul and the transmission of original sin, and it is no accident that this new interest coincides with both the expanding debate over the status of universals and the gradual introduction of works of medicine and natural science translated from the Arabic.[139] Anselm of Canterbury, perhaps the best-known orthodox dialectician from the eleventh century, discusses the reception and consequences of original sin in his *De conceptu virginali et originali peccato*.[140] In the process, he employs a philosophical vocabulary that distinguishes nature from person and natural sin from personal sin. He fails to decide between the virtues of traducianism or creationism, however. This failure evidently disturbed him for the rest of his life. Eadmer, in his *Vita Anselmi*, notes that when Anselm was near death he expressed a hope that he might have a little more time in this world in order to solve the problem of the origin of the soul, a problem which he had been turning over and over in his mind and which he feared no one after him would solve.[141]

The most complete eleventh-century treatment of traducianism and creationism, however, comes not from the better known schools of Laon or Bec but from Tournai. In his little-known *De peccato originali*, Odo presents the first theological treatise written expressly on original sin since Augustine.[142] This work represents an important part of a long theological struggle moving to define the origin of the soul and the transmission of original sin.[143] Moreover, it displays Odo's optimistic assessment, characteristic of the twelfth-century renaissance, that a problem which no less an authority than Pope Gregory I had declared beyond any solution[144] might yet yield its secrets to philosophical investigation. This optimism is also reflected in the "authorities" Odo employs in his treatise. Although he does quote Scripture when necessary, his primary authority appears to have been philosophical reason itself. This expectation that philosophical argument may yet unravel the secrets of a theological mystery again reflects the spirit of the twelfth-century renaissance.

It is not clear whether Odo's text was written before or after Anselm's *De conceptu virginali et originali peccato*, which Anselm composed between the summer of 1099 and the summer of 1100.[145] Odo's treatise was likely written sometime between 1095 and 1105, although Julius Gross suggests a date as late as 1110.[146] Odo himself gives us only a single clue to help establish a date of composition. In the prologue to *De peccato originali* Odo explains that he has reluctantly agreed to treat the thorny problem of original sin only after other monks prevailed on him, arguing that now he has time because he has been freed from external cares. Gross likely assumes that since Odo retired from the bishopric of Cambrai to Anchin in 1110 he wrote the text then, when he was freed from episcopal cares. But, as has been shown, Odo was relieved of all but spiritual duties at St. Martin of Tournai by early 1096, although he remained abbot. It seems equally probable, then, that Odo would have written the text between 1096–1105, before he was elected Bishop of Cambrai. An earlier date seems more likely if one assumes that Odo wrote *De peccato originali* before its companion work, the *Disputatio contra Judaeum Leonem nomine de adventu Christi filii Dei*, written probably in 1105 or 1106. If systematic theology follows a certain logic, one would expect a treatment of original sin before a discussion of the necessity of the Incarnation. Greater precision in establishing the date of composition seems impossible to attain at this time.

If Odo wrote *De peccato originali* before 1099, there arises the intriguing possibility that Odo's treatise antedates Anselm's and that Anselm may have been Odo's "disciple" (in some sense). Both authors share the view that original sin is the result of the loss of original justice that Adam enjoyed.[147] Moreover, Odo shares Anselm's understanding of adequate satisfaction, found in Anselm's *Cur Deus Homo*, which identifies the satisfaction of the God-Man as necessary to remove the stain of original sin.[148] These similarities have led most historians to conclude that Odo must have been one of Anselm's students or disciples.[149] Since it is not certain that Odo wrote his work after Anselm's, however, it also cannot be determined that it was Anselm who influenced Odo and not the other way around.[150] Moreover, it is not even clear that Odo and Anselm agree on the most probable philosophical solution to the problem of the transmission of original sin, especially if we accept the apparent traducianism of Gilbert Crispin, one of Anselm's students, as Anselm's own.[151] Odo adopts the creationist solution,[152] and it is creationism which ultimately is established in the later Middle Ages as the doctrine of the Church.

As part of his defense of creationism, Odo makes it clear that Tertullian's material traducianism is indefensible.[153] This doctrine maintained that original sin is conveyed with the seed of the body from one generation to the next, from the parent to the child. But it had been argued by Augustine and others that sin pertains to the soul and to the rational will in particular and not to the body. It cannot be inherited, then, in the same way that physical attributes are inherited.

Yet spiritual traducianism, a more subtle modification of material traducianism, offered many attractive features. This view proposed that each soul is generated from a parent soul "as light is kindled from light," just as each body is generated from the body of the parent. The popularity of this view benefited from the fact that procreation provided a powerful model from ordinary experience in order to explain both the sense in which all are "in" Adam, and the way in which sin is transmitted from Adam to later generations. Spiritual traducianists argued that just as my body is "in" Adam and descends from his, so too analogously my soul is "in" Adam and descends from his alongside the seed of the flesh. Certain physical resemblances in later generations can be explained according to this model, whereby the body of the child is produced by the separation of the material seed from the body of the parent. The seed is implanted in the womb, is nourished there, and develops into a human body. It forms a link in a chain, one generation after the next, retreating even to the first parent. In the same way, certain moral or psychological dispositions can be explained by the hypothesis that the soul of each child is contained virtually or in some other way in the soul of the parent and, ultimately, in the soul of the first parent. This would seem to solve the problem of the transmission of original sin: just as each human body is generated from a seed separated from Adam's body, so every soul is generated from a "seed" separated from Adam's soul and bears the sin that its parent soul contracted, as well as the same inclination toward sin, that is concupiscence. This approach may also have converged with the incipient nominalism appearing at the end of the eleventh century. For those who were unable to assign real existence to the universal nature, namely the soul nature human beings share, it may have been easier to accept a solution that proposed that individual souls are only generated from prior individuals.

While spiritual traducianism promised to solve the problem of the origin of the soul and the transmission of original sin, it suffered from seemingly insuperable philosophical difficulties, of which Odo was well aware. If the soul is a spiritual substance, without parts or material extension, then how can we understand the *separation* of one soul from another? This is a problem Odo does not believe traducianism can overcome. Moreover, Odo turns on its head the very model of procreation which traducianism finds so useful to describe the transmission of the soul from parent to child. *His* observations of nature focus upon the fact that the root-stock or seed (*semen*) that produces later generations in both plants and animals is of a different species than either parent or child.[154] But how, then, can something which has a different substance than the soul transmit or convey the soul to posterity? Despite its theological advantages, the philosophical difficulties attendant upon spiritual traducianism led Odo to look for another solution.

That solution, the one he claims is the orthodox view (although without citing a single orthodox defender), is creationism. It is a doctrine that holds that God creates each soul from nothing and infuses it into a body that is generated from a seed descending from our first parent. The body, then, is a link in a chain; the soul is new for each individual. While this seemed to solve one problem, it produced many others. The most powerful objection, Odo recognizes, is this: "if I have only the body from Adam, and the soul truly is not from Adam but from God alone, and since sin is only in the soul and not in the body, then how can I say that I have sinned in Adam?"[155] Just as important, if God creates each soul from nothing and introduces it to the body, is not God then responsible for the fact that it enters the body with sin? Is not God guilty of having created a corrupt and deformed soul?

Even though Odo attempts to dispatch these problems quickly, he struggles with the nature of the created soul. For him, it is especially the rational soul that constitutes the human being. But if each soul is created from nothing, is the soul radically individual or is there a universal human soul (something we may call the species nature) which somehow unites us all? Odo is convinced that there is a universal nature which is properly the human and fully real. The soul of the individual, then, participates (in a manner not clearly envisioned) in the universal nature. But if the soul is universal as well as individual, and if Adam sinned as an individual, the difficulty of explaining how his sin can be communicated to other individual souls remains.

These are merely some of the difficulties that Odo encounters. In themselves they were sufficient to lead him to undertake an extensive discussion of the nature and origin of the soul in *De peccato originali*. This discussion utilizes a philosophical vocabulary that can create real problems for the translator. How should one translate Latin terms like *res*, *substantia*, *esse*, *forma*, *figura*, and *species*? One might examine their use in comparison with the work of other contemporary, or nearly contemporary, Latin authors for some guidance. *Substantia*, *figura*, and *forma*, among others, were philosophical terms crucial to the eucharistic controversy surrounding Berengar of Tours. One of the achievements of this controversy was to give these terms greater precision.[156] Odo himself contributed to this process with his *Exposition on the Canon of the Mass*.[157] But in *De peccato originali* Odo attempts himself to define his philosophical terminology with precision, making a comparative study unnecessary for the translator, even though it may be of critical importance for the historian. In this translation, I have simply attempted to employ Odo's own definitions consistently. Ultimately, however, no translation can capture all the nuances of this vocabulary.

Disputation with the Jew, Leo, Concerning the Advent of Christ, the Son of God

This text bears a close theological relationship to Odo's *On Original Sin*. If the latter demonstrates the inevitable pollution of the individual nature with the sin of Adam, the *Disputatio contra Judaeum Leonem nomine de adventu Christi filii Dei* will attempt to prove that only the God-Man can remove that pollution and effect human redemption.[158] The post-lapsarian human condition, then, "necessitates" the Incarnation and Atonement.[159]

Odo's treatise, written in the form of a dialogue, was completed during his episcopate (probably in 1105 or 1106) and is addressed to Acard, a monk of Fémy.[160] In his prologue, Odo discloses that he had first presented the theme of this dialogue in a sermon[161] just before the Feast of the Nativity. Later, Acard was unable to remember its details and prevailed upon Odo to write down the things he had said then as an aid to memory. Odo chose the dialogue as the form for his discussion because, he says, he actually had an encounter and discussion with a Jew when he had attended a council at Poitiers (the council was held on 18 November 1100) and had been called upon to dispatch some business involving this Jew and the community of Senlis.[162] Indeed, Odo is perhaps the first witness to the existence of a Jewish community at Senlis, a town in the Oise department of northern France — a Jewish community whose economic resources apparently far exceeded its numbers.[163]

Although Odo was on his way to a council treating issues related to the crusade, at a time when some were using the crusading fervor to encourage attacks against Jewish communities in Europe a remarkable feature of this dialogue is that it avoids invective and sustains an irenic tone.[164] Moreover, as in his *De peccato originali*, Odo does not rely as much upon argument based on scriptural authority as he does upon the evidence that reason alone provides.[165] But this need not imply that Odo's work was merely a literary or theological exercise, one not rooted in an historical encounter. On the contrary, the evidence suggests that it did grow out of a real encounter.[166] Unlike so many of the Christian literary "dialogues" with Jews, a genre that too often merely provides for a polemical expression of Christian anti-Judaism, Odo's dialogue seems genuine.[167] Leo is not at all the straw man so common in this controversial literature, which expanded dramatically in the twelfth century.[168] His presentation of Jewish teaching is, as Dahan agrees, reasonably authentic.[169] At the same time, Jewish objections present real challenges for Odo and, evidently, for other Catholics as well. Odo remarks at the end of this work that he has written it down especially for those Catholics who had become "lost" among the arguments of Jews. These arguments were likely familiar to Odo's contemporaries from older Christian polemics against Judaism, dating from as early as the second century (e.g., Justin Martyr's *Dialogue with Trypho*). Yet there is also now a possibility that Odo's contemporaries were becoming aware of Jewish arguments from Jewish polemical literature against Christianity, which begins to appear only in the ninth or tenth century within Jewish communities under the protection of Islam, and from actual encounters and discussions like the one Odo had himself.[170]

It is impossible to determine whether those to whom Odo referred as having become "lost" among Jewish arguments should be identified as "judaizing" Christians (that is, either naive theological opponents or determined sectarian Christians) or Christian converts to Judaism. The phenomenon of Christian conversion to Judaism during the Middle Ages often goes unacknowledged. Although it is true that at this time the conversion of Christians to Judaism was both a dangerous and rare undertaking, it was not for that reason unknown. Indeed, the discovery at the turn of the twentieth century of the Cairo *Geniza*, a storehouse for Hebrew documents in the synagogue of Old Cairo, has illuminated the personal histories of two prominent churchmen from western Europe who had become Jewish converts about the time Odo composed his *Disputation*. In the *Genizah* was found the *Scroll of Obadiah*, which contains the autobiography of Obadiah the Norman (a Roman Catholic priest who abandoned Christianity for Judaism soon after the first crusade) and provides information about the conversion to Judaism of Andreas, Archbishop of Bari, about the beginning of the twelfth century. These two churchmen figure prominently in Bernhard Blumenkranz's portrait of Christian clergy of the late eleventh or early twelfth century who converted to Judaism.[171]

The Archbishop of Bari, Andreas, abandoned the wealth and prestige of his archepiscopal position, evidently from compassion for Jewish suffering during the first crusade, and traveled to Constantinople, where he was circumcized. When his conversion became known, he himself became the subject of persecution. Apostasy was a serious crime subject to the authority of both the Church and Christian rulers. Andreas was placed in prison and threatened with death if he did not renounce his new religious identity and revert to the Christian faith. Instead, Andreas apparently succeeded in convincing his persecutor of the superiority of Judaism and obtained from him an opportunity for escape. He traveled to Cairo and, according to the *Scroll of Obadiah*, he composed there some fourteen treatises defending Judaism. These he sent to the highest dignitaries of the Church. Some of them were clearly intended to serve as guides that would lead Christians to Judaism, along the path he had himself taken.

In part it was the personal example of Andreas that was most persuasive for Obadiah the Norman. Born ca. 1070 to a prominent aristocratic Christian family in Oppido Lucano (Italy) he was given the name John. His twin brother Roger was destined for a military career as a knight and warrior, but Obadiah was destined for the Church. Shortly after pronouncing his vows as a priest he began to consider the merits of Judaism. As in the case of Andreas, he may have felt a compelling sense of compassion for the sufferings of Jewish communities at the hands of the Crusaders. Assisted by the community of Frankish Jews, he fled to the East, leaving Europe for Constantinople, where he may have begun his study of Judaism in earnest. From there he moved to Baghdad, where he studied the Hebrew Bible. Later he traveled to Aleppo, where in 1113 he received a letter of recommendation from R. Baruch b. Isaac, the *rosh yeshiva*, verifying his conversion. Finally, after a journey to Palestine, he traveled to Egypt and settled around Cairo, where, it is presumed, he died. Like Andreas of Bari, Obadiah composed literature for Christians intended to persuade them of the superiority of Judaism.[172]

While it is impossible to demonstrate that Odo wrote with these two in mind, it is possible that he was aware of them. The example of prominent Christian clergy who became Jews would likely have earned some notice. Consequently, one may reasonably infer both that Odo's *Disputation* arose from a real historical encounter with a Jew and that his intended audience, that is, Christians (or Christian converts to Judaism) who had become lost among Jewish claims, was equally real. For these reasons, this work cannot be dismissed as a mere exercise in theological polemics.

If it were an exercise in theological polemics one would expect that, at its end, Leo would gratefully acknowledge the truth of Odo's arguments and rush forward toward baptism. In fact, nothing of the sort occurs. Although Leo admits that Odo's claims are stronger than he anticipated, he still refuses to embrace Christianity. Arguments alone, Leo suggests, are not enough to convince him. Nevertheless, Odo's arguments were evidently respected by the next generation of medieval theologians and were cited alongside those Anselm supplied in his *Cur Deus Homo*.[173]

The use of this text by medieval theologians alongside *Cur Deus Homo* raises again the vexing problem of the literary and historical relationship between the two works and their authors. Both texts are dialogues. Both treat the Christian understanding of the Incarnation and Atonement. Both are written near the beginning of the twelfth century.[174] Although they bear many similarities, it would be a mistake to regard Odo's work as a truncated version of Anselm's *Cur Deus Homo*. In the first place, Odo's treatise is a dialogue with a Jew; Anselm's treatise is a dialogue with a Christian disciple.[175] Apart from this formal difference, Anselm addresses issues that Odo never takes up: for example, the classical or ransom theory of the Atonement, which Anselm replaces with a theory of satisfaction or substitutionary Atonement. Moreover, Anselm clearly defines the nature of sin, of which all but the God-Man is guilty, as a failure to render to God his due.[176] This insult to God's honor imposes a debt which only the God-Man can repay.[177]

Odo never explicitly identifies sin as a failure to render honor to God. Nor is he interested in examining various theories of the Atonement. His primary concern is to show Leo that for any sin whatsoever, although we may obtain *forgiveness* for sin under the Law, it is not possible to render *satisfaction* for sin without the God-Man. Without satisfaction, mankind can never enter heaven and replace the fallen angels. Consequently, without satisfaction, God's plan for creation must remain incomplete and frustrated. Since this is impossible, satisfaction is necessary. While Anselm emphasizes that the demands of divine justice require satisfaction, Odo emphasizes the demands of divine providence. The shift may be subtle, but it provides a different orientation for the two works.

While these differences in form and content may at least suggest that when writing this work Odo was not directly dependent upon Anselm, Herman's silence on this point may be even more telling. In a letter to Stephen, the archbishop of Vienna, in which Herman mentions his own composition on the Incarnation, he explains that he used both Anselm's *Cur Deus Homo* and Odo's sermon on the Incarnation (to which Odo refers in the prologue to the *Disputation*) when writing his work.[178] Herman does not, however, indicate that Odo was in any way indebted to Anselm for his discussion of the Incarnation, as one might expect if Anselm enjoyed the position of master and Odo that of disciple.

Texts and Editions

With the exception of Odo's *Exposition on the Canon of the Mass*, none of his works has been translated or has appeared in a critical edition.[179] For my translation of Odo's *On Original Sin* and his *Disputation with the Jew, Leo, Concerning the Advent of Christ, the Son of God* I have compared the edition in Migne's *Patrologia* (volume 160, cols. 1071–1102; 1103–1112) with the printed text on which it is based in the older *Maxima bibliotheca veterum Patrum*.[180] I then compared these with copies of two twelfth-century codices. The first, Douai Bibl. mun. 201 (fols. 64–70; 92–112) contains both *On Original Sin* and the *Disputation with the Jew*. This parchment manuscript probably originated at the abbey of Anchin, where Odo died. In the late sixteenth century it likely passed to the abbey of Marchiennes, near Tournai, where it may have been recopied. The manuscript contains in red the headings and divisions of the text indicated in this translation (and present also in the printed editions).

Although at the conclusion to his *Exposition on the Canon of the Mass* Odo provides copyists or scribes with instructions to observe the original divisions, punctuation, and chapter headings he has placed in that text,[181] an examination of Douai Bibl. mun. 201 suggests that the chapter headings and divisions in *On Original Sin* have been added later. This is evident from the fact that the headings have been inserted into the text, sometimes extending into the margins. If they had been present in Odo's original, the copyist would have left the rubricator room for the chapter headings. Although these headings are probably not original to the work, they have been retained here in order to assist the reader who wishes to consult the Latin text. Similarly, the chart on p. 72 below and which attempts to provide a graphic representation of the relationship between genera and species is found as a marginal addition to Douai Bibl. mun. 201, and reproduced in Migne's printed edition. It has been included here as an illustration which, if not original to Odo's work, was understood by later readers to be of some assistance.

The second codex, Troyes Bibl. mun. 398 (fols. 83–85),[182] provides another copy of the *Disputation with the Jew*. I have also examined Harvard

University's MS Judaica 16, which contains a slightly truncated text of this disputation from a German manuscript of the middle of the fifteenth century. Here again one can assume that the chapter headings or divisions in the work, found in the printed editions, are not original. In Troyes Bibl. mun. 398 they again appear to have been inserted, sometimes extending into the margin. It also may be instructive that Harvard University's MS Judaica 16, while a later copy, does not contain these headings at all. The dialogue form, however, in which the speaker is identified throughout the text, is present in both manuscript copies and is certainly original to Odo's composition.

Finally, deletions or insertions are clearly evident in our manuscripts, especially in Douai Bibl. mun. 201 and Harvard MS Judaica 16. The latter is missing not only the last fifteen lines of the work as printed in Migne (PL 160: 1112C) but also a large section between cols. 1110D and 1111C. While Douai Bibl. mun. 201 provides a text of *On Original Sin* that is largely identical to what is found in Migne's edition, two substantial corrections and additions are apparent in the manuscript. In the first, at fol. 103^r the top eleven lines have been crossed out and a partial leaf, now numbered 102$^{r/v}$ has replaced them. This addition seems to go on at greater length than the original, and gives the text found in Migne (PL 160: 1085–86). Later, at fol. 107^r, an insertion sign in the manuscript directs the reader to an added manuscript slip. This adds eight lines to the manuscript, providing the form found in Migne (PL 160: 1093). Finally, at the bottom of 108^r it appears that a slip has been added which introduces the first six lines of the section entitled "On Figure" (PL 160: 1097D–1098A). These lines seem out of place here, however. The same material is repeated again, at somewhat greater length, at 109^r and then follows the order of the text presented in Migne. These alterations appear to be in the same hand that has produced the rest of the manuscript. Although one might want to dismiss them as corrections required by scribal errors and omissions, it is also possible that these alterations may reflect changes Odo himself (or members of his community) wanted introduced to the text. Again, Douai Bibl. mun. 201 is a twelfth-century copy from Anchin, where Odo died. It is at least possible that it dates from before his death.

When Migne's edition does depart from these early manuscripts, I have often preferred these to Migne's text in order to preserve the sense of the work. When I have chosen an alternative reading, I have made a note and suggested emendation. Although the printed text which appears in the *Maxima bibliotheca veterum Patrum* and later in Migne's edition may have utilized manuscripts which have since been lost or destroyed, for us Douai Bibl. mun. 201 represents the oldest codex extant containing Odo's works. It is this codex which was employed as the base for a recent critical edition of Odo's *Exposition on the Canon of the Mass*,[183] against which more than a dozen other copies were checked. I am reasonably confident, then, that the text on which this translation is based is sound.

On Original Sin

Book I

Prologue

I shall speak about the often discussed question of original sin, which frequently is raised among the orthodox;[1] I call upon you, O Holy Spirit, to assist me, guarding my mind and my speech in all things, lest something arise in this project that does not please you. I beg the brothers not to accuse me of presumption because I strive to discuss a matter very frequently debated but never really examined, and strive to shed a little new light upon an ancient confusion. Certain brothers have urged me to do this. They pressed me, excused from occupation with external things,[2] to guard against the charge of burying my talent (cf. Matt. 25: 26; Lk. 19: 12). When I excused myself by claiming a dull nature they answered me with this passage from the psalms: "Open your mouth and I will fill it (Ps. 80: 11, Vulg.)." I feared the difficulty of the question, and they responded with God's promise, saying: "I have laid help upon one that is mighty (Ps. 88: 20, Vulg.)." And I thought to myself that many times things I did not understand became clear to me while I was writing. Overcome, then, by the unceasing prayers of the brothers and by that love which, when it burns, often exceeds every measure, and trusting in God's mercy and the aid of the brothers' prayers, I descended into the dark pit. I entered into the hidden recesses of this difficult question, hoping to derive light from the darkness. One must know that this question of original sin is derived from what the apostle [Paul] said: "In whom all have sinned (Rom. 5: 12)," that is to say, in Adam. But it is asked: how have we sinned in Adam, drawing the origin of sin from Adam? Yet before we may set forth the difficult points of this question it seems one ought to ask what it is that is called sin.

In what ways is something called evil

Sin, then, is the evil which God does not make. Now, something is called evil in two ways—namely, the evil that God makes, and the evil that God does not make. For this reason it is written: "Making peace and creating evil (Isa. 45: 7)";[3] and, "if there is evil in the city, God has not made it (Amos 3: 6)." For God makes punishment for sins, which is evil to those suffering it, and God requites evils for sin. God in no wise creates that evil, however, which is called injustice; rather, he punishes it, so that he is in no way the author of that which he punishes.

That sin is not in the body

This evil of injustice is not found in our bodies nor do we say properly that we sin by the body. Now, in the act of murder what is called evil? If you accuse the sword of being evil, God has made the steel. If you accuse the hand, even that God has made. If you accuse the motion of the hand, or of the sword, who is ignorant of the fact that motion has an essence? If there is an essence, it is made by God, for every essence except God himself is made by God. The motion that God has made is not, then, evil. Thus, neither is the soul of man itself an evil which God has not made. If then neither the soul, nor the steel of the sword, nor the hand, nor the motion is evil at all, what then is said to be evil in murder? In no way is evil found in corporeal things. Similarly, in adultery neither is the person, nor the sex, nor the motion, nor the flux,[4] nor the sexual desire itself an evil, which God has not made. Finally, the very corporeal things which God has made are not the evil, which God has not made. Nor is evil in them so that they thereby might rightly be called evil. So, if someone should accuse bodies of evil because they perform adultery, quite rightly they can excuse themselves. By the disposition of the creator we are subject to the soul for as long as we are animated by it. The Lord placed it in us; let us serve it and obey it in all things.[5] We are moved to all things, then, at its command by divine ordination. How, then, by obeying reason, just as God commanded, do we sin? We commit adultery, but mistress reason commanded, and we were unable to resist her command. Thus has God ordained, and consequently we are not evildoers when doing evil.[6] Nor are we evil because we do something evil,[7] because we do not do our own evil but someone else's. Praise the obedient servant, and fault the lord who commands. How does a horse sin when it carries an enemy? How does a lance sin when it wounds a man?

That sin is in the rational soul alone

Truly, he errs who looks for sin in the body, for it is found nowhere else than in a rational spirit and its will. Nevertheless, neither reason nor the will nor the spirit itself is an evil, which God has not made. Rather, the injustice of the will is the evil that we seek, for in no way has God made that injustice, and it is an evil that ought not to be imputed to God. Nor should we seek a [single] author of all evils, such as God is known to be the author of all goods.[8]

That evil is a positive reality according to the Manichaeans

The heresy of the Manichaeans,[9] thinking that evil is an essence, affirmed this view because they see evil divided, just like a genus, into a number of species. They argue that along with the evil of injustice there may be pride, fornication, and many other species [of evil] subsumed beneath a genus, and we may see subdivisions of such species descend in order as far as individuals.[10] Conversely, several individuals may in reality be united in one species, and several species in one genus. In like manner, are not the higher things [such as genera] most fittingly predicated of their inferiors? Who would deny that there is a substance whereby one answers the question, "what" [is it]? Who will deny that it has an essence, when he will not deny that there is a universal?

Here is another Manichaean argument (*Aliter*). Every noun signifies something according to convention.[11] And who will deny that this word — that is, evil — is a noun, which the grammarian says is of a simple figure; that it is declined through all cases; and that it may be singular or plural in number? Therefore, it signifies something according to convention. A Greek-speaker and a Latin-speaker hear this [same] word. To the Greek who hears it, it is only a sound, and he understands nothing by it. If the Latin-speaker does not plainly deceive him, as he says he does,[12] let him examine his conscience, and he will find that the word affects his mind. Because surely when this word is heard it conveys some significance to the mind of the Latin-speaker. For when he hears he is doing "evil," either he denies it or agrees, which the one who does not understand the word does not do. Since therefore that word is a noun, it signifies something; if something, then an essence, for what does not have an essence is not something. What is called evil, then, is an essence and evil is not nothing.[13] The Manichaeans defend the view that evil has an essence and is something existing with just such arguments. By these they are driven to their heresy, and to assert that there is a creator of all evils.[14]

That evil is nothing

On the other hand, we say that evil is nothing existent and has no essence. Now, whatever God has not made is nothing. However, God has not made evil. He who has made everything that is evil, therefore, is nothing and has no essence. If something exists, God — who makes all that is — has made it. But it is wicked to say that God has made anything evil. Therefore, evil is nothing, because evil is a privation of good, and everyone who understands rightly knows that a privation is not something.[15]

Finally, there are four modes of opposition, that is of contraries and of relations: affirmation, negation, privation, and possession (*habitus*).[16] The first of these contraries and relatives oppose one thing to another, like white to black, which are opposed as contraries. Each exists, and each one has its essence. Similarly lord and servant, which are relatives: each one exists, and each one has a true essence. The two remaining modes of opposition[17] oppose that which does not exist to something that does, for example when not-man is opposed to man as a negation. Indeed a man is; a not-man, truly, is without an essence. Similarly, when impious is opposed to pious as a privation, piety is; impiety truly is without an essence and is only the privation of essence. Just as not-man only denies the existence of a man, thus also impiety denies the existence of piety. However that which only denies being cannot be; therefore neither can a privation or negation have an essence. Now, evil therefore does not exist if it is only a privation of good. But it is only a privation of good. Because good and evil are predicated in many ways, in order to show this more clearly — lest ambiguity introduce error — let us select justice as a good and injustice as an evil, if only because we have proposed to speak about sin, which we have called an injustice and an evil.

That privation is nothing

Injustice, then, is the privation of justice, since indeed the privatory particle only removes justice and does not posit another essence. Just as "not," a negative adverb, denies that the appositive exists and does not posit another essence,[18] so too the privatory particle "in" removes the essence placed in apposition, but does not posit another essence. Now, just as "not-just" denies that the appositive "just" is present but does not posit another essence, so too injustice removes justice but does not posit another essence. A privation differs from a negation only in this respect, that there is a negation everywhere the thing negated does not exist. A privation, however, does not exist everywhere that the privative[19] does not exist, but only where the privative ought to exist. Neither is there ever a privation without the absence of the privative.[20] Nor can we properly speak of a privation when the privative does not have to exist. Consequently, irrational is not properly predicated of something which is not supposed to have the use of reason. Sometimes, however, privations are [improperly] used instead of negations and, when names for things are lacking, privations are often used as substitutes for these things themselves. However, we only treat here privation, as it is properly called. Since therefore the privation of justice is injustice, there is no essence [of injustice] and for that reason injustice is nothing. Therefore, sin and evil are nothing, since sin and evil are nothing but injustice.

That evils do not have species or genera[21]

Thus, evil is not a genus. Nor are there species into which it may be divided — such as adultery, homicide, etc. — since evil and these species do not have an essence. Now, that which does not have an essence is not a genus, a species, a universal, or a particular.

That an understanding of evils proceeds from an understanding of goods

There is an ascending or descending order found among evils that parallels the hierarchy of good things. Obviously, whatever we say of privations we draw entirely from things lacking [some quality]. Privation does not produce anything unless the basis for the privation comes first, nor can we produce a privation unless we have a thing which is lacking [some quality]. Therefore, the species and genera of things come first, with the result that we judge the different types of privations according to them. For unless we shall have first known the essences of justice, patience, and piety we cannot understand their privations: injustice, impatience, and impiety.

Truth exists in the essences of genera and species, whereas its imitation [is found] in privations, just as in negations. In the latter there are obviously no essences, or genera, or species. It is rather the opposite: from the very essences of the things negated these assume the likeness of genera and the appearance of species, but not their truth.[22] For just as man is a species under the genus animal, so too not-animal is just like a species under not-man. And this is what Boethius calls contraposition in the first part of [Aristotle's] *Categories*.[23] This contraposition is not, however, the truth of species or genera, but its imitation.[24] Just as this is the case for negations, so it is also the case for privations. But it is obvious that there is only imitation in negations. In privations it is not so obvious, however, because they are so much more like existing things, to such an extent that many people think that they *are* things and have their own proper essence, because they are only predicated of those things in which the privative ought to be, and is not. Moreover, privations have their own nouns, sometimes without privative particles, just like essences.[25] Negations never have their own nouns without a negative particle, nor do they admit that what they lack ought to exist; rather, negations are predicated of all things in which the thing negated is not found, the way that not-man is everything which is not a man.[26] But an unjust person truly does not exist unless one who ought to be just, is not just.

That the nouns of a privation and a possession signify the same thing

Privations, however, very often have nouns without privative particles just like a possession (*habitus*)[27] does — evil, just like good, darkness just like light, blindness just like sight, fornication just like chastity. And although the privation of an essence does not set up an opposite essence because there is no essence for a privation, nevertheless the noun standing for a privation does not signify its own essence, but the essence of the *habitus*. Therefore, the noun for the privation and the noun for the *habitus* signify the same thing. But a *habitus* has its own noun, while the noun of a privation signifies another's noun. A *habitus* signifies its own essence by positing something, while the noun of a privation signifies the same thing by denying something. The noun of a *habitus* makes present that which you understand, while the noun for a privation takes away from what you understand. The noun of a privation is, then, significative of something, but not of its own substance (*suae rei*);[28] rather, it is significative of another thing which it signifies as something that is lacking some quality.

Epilogue

From the foregoing, one can infer that evil is in the rational spirit alone. It is not a reality in a subject, but the denial of a reality in a subject. When you say that evil is in the will, you do not mean that it is something existing in the will; you only mean that a good is absent from where it ought to be. Plainly it is an evil that this good is not present where it ought to be, because injustice is justice that is not where it ought to be, and he is unjust who is not just when he ought to be. What can be said more correctly than that he is unjust who was unwilling to hold onto the justice given to him when he could have, and freely abandoned the gift of such a great good?

That a rational nature cannot be without the justice that it should have

You have received justice — a good entrusted to us — which ought to be carefully guarded. It should even be given back [to the giver], because the one who entrusted us with the deposit wants it back. Do you wish to make a return of it properly? Then guard it well. For the more you guard, the more you will give back; and the more you will give back, the more you will keep.[29] Justice is a marvelous good which you give back [to the giver] while guarding it, and while giving it back you do not lose it. But by returning more, more do you guard. The good, I say, ought to be guarded with all your strength so that you may return it, because if you lose it you do not have what you should return. Nevertheless, you are endebted for this deposit to the one who entrusted it to you. He entrusted it, therefore you owe it. But perhaps you have lost it voluntarily because freely you abandoned it. Still, he requires the deposit which he gave you. You do not have it because voluntarily you have lost what you ought to return. He who gave it is found, then, to be a just creditor; you, who do not return it, an unjust debtor. Unjust, I say, not because you would have some essence in this privation, but because you do not have the essence of justice that you ought to have, and it is required because you received it and did not guard it, but freely deserted it.[30] Thus arises the error of the Manichaeans who, thinking that evil is a real essence that they could not attribute to a good god, were compelled to imagine an author for all evils, so that there were two opposing authors of contrary things: namely a good author for goods and an evil one for evils. Thus, they affirmed two first principles of all things.

That he is not punished for nothing who is punished for evil

Perhaps someone will say: what then? If evil is nothing, we are punished for nothing when we are punished for evil.[31] And it seems stupid to argue about injustice if indeed injustice is without an essence. But if those things said of privations are thoughtfully considered no one will be moved by this [apparent] opposition, for without a *habitus* a privation can neither be expressed nor understood, nor is a privation anything other than the absence of some due quality, as injustice is the absence of justice. Therefore, when we are punished for injustice we are punished for having abandoned justice. But as justice is something, we are punished for something. So when injustice is said to be nothing, nevertheless something is understood by that: something for which we are punished because we have deserted it. We are punished then for the justice we have deserted. So too a privation is nothing, but, when we are punished for it, we are punished for that which is something. Most justly he who gave that which was always to be kept punishes the one who freely abandoned it. He punishes indeed because of justice, not because it is "had" but because it is not had; not, then, because it is present but because it is absent.[32] But when justice is absent, it is injustice. Therefore injustice appears when justice is not where it ought to be. But [injustice] signifies that justice does not exist where it ought to exist; nor does it signify that justice exists where it ought not to exist. Therefore, injustice does not signify that something exists, since it only denies that justice exists, although only in those cases where it ought to exist. But say that injustice posits something that really exists "and have Phyllis to yourself."[33]

That essences are said of non-existents

But perhaps someone says: of course we say that injustice is a privation and an opposite and a relation. No one of sound mind will deny that a privation and an opposite and a relation exist because a privation and an opposite are species of the most general genus [or category] of relation.[34] How then is injustice said not to exist when so many essences are predicated of it? Now, if something is predicated of anything, then it exists. Otherwise, something could be predicated of what does not exist.[35]

Yet assuredly a thing can be predicated of something that does not exist, both by convention and through necessity.[36] Often it is necessary for us to speak of things which do not exist; because they lack their own names (*voces*) we use names of things that exist [in order to speak of them]. And because we cannot talk about them using their own proper names we are compelled to talk about them using the names of other things. For look, when we fix upon many things in thought, images (*figurae*)[37] are formed in the mind, but the things which they represent are not found there. Thought, indeed, appropriates images from things that exist, but it fashions them for those that do not exist. The mind cannot think of what does not exist, unless it fashions forms (*formas*) from that which does exist, so that through the forms of things that exist, it may think of things that do not. While we say that we are thinking them, just as the mind is unable to contemplate what does not exist unless it conforms to a likeness of something that does, so too language cannot describe things which do not exist except by using terms for things which do. For speech follows thought, so that language does not use words differently than thought orders images. So, a painter is unable to paint things that do not exist except by using images of things that do. He paints things which do not exist in the physical world by using those forms which thought, in a mental world, dictates from those things which do exist.[38] It is common to appeal to a certain proverb when discussing and painting what does not exist — "Painters and Poets have always had an equal right in venturing anything"[39] — and whenever we wish to recount the images found in dreams and describe the foolish thoughts of sleep, how can their ephemeral nature be described if not through the words of real things? It is not strange, then, that when we speak of privations we employ words of existing things for them, and provide a basis[40] for privations through the names of existing things.

That each one is the author of his own evil

Before we return to our task, something else arises that can confuse the reader if it has not been resolved. Now, because it is said against the Manichaeans that there is no author of all evils, perhaps someone may entertain some doubt and say: where does evil come from if no one is the author of all evils? But truth reveals that each one is the author of his own evil. Although you may have sinned because of bad example, or because someone urged you on, or because of compulsion, still the sin that you have done belongs to you, who have done it. No necessity could compel you, unless you willed it. Remove the will and you will see that no necessity has power [to compel you to evil]. Would you fall upon someone or murder him? It does not happen unless you will it. It is not by necessity, then, that you sin, but by the will alone. And likewise it is the will alone that is punished or rewarded. It is punished if you suffer what you do not want; it is rewarded if you achieve what you properly willed. You are then the very author of your own evil. You, who have sinned by the desire of your own will may not ascribe to others what you yourself have done, nor seek another author. You have made yourself the responsible agent.[41] But now that we have brought these inquiries to an end, let us rest for a moment, so that refreshed by this rest we may rise up with more energy from this book to the ones following.

Book II

The double source for original sin[42]

It has been our intention to discuss original sin, since one asks how we may have sin from our very origin, that is from Adam and Eve. This question arises from what one reads in the [epistle of the] Apostle: "In whom all have sinned (Rom. 5: 12)."

Consequently, one asks: how have we sinned in Adam? It is true that we were all in Adam and arise from him, but according to the flesh. But the authority of the orthodox Fathers says something else about the soul. For it does not propose that a soul has been engendered from a soul just as the flesh is engendered from flesh; nor does it propose that a part is separated from a soul, from which another man's spirit comes into existence just as a part is separated from the flesh, from which the body of another man comes into existence.[43] Nevertheless, there are many who think that the soul comes from a "root-stock" (*ex traduce*) just as the body does, and that the power of the soul issues with the seed of the body. We should examine each of their reasons as we have introduced them, because it seems they ought not to be spurned in every sense.[44] But first let us pursue the path of the orthodox.

Why God is said to have rested from labor if even now he creates souls from nothing

This is their doctrine[45] concerning the human soul: that nothing is separated from the parent's soul with the seed of the progeny, nor is anything ever drawn from the parent's soul to the child's soul, nor does a soul following after derive something from one that already exists. Rather, just as God breathed a new soul into the first man, thus always does he breathe new souls into new bodies. New, I say, and fresh: either newly made from some secret and hidden existents, or newly created just as in the beginning all creation was created from nothing.

The passage in Genesis (Gen. 2: 2) where God is said to have rested from all the work he had been doing is thrown up against them, just as though a sort of fatigue from begetting [souls] daily were not compatible with [his] rest from the work of creation, or as though he is not truly said to rest from those things which he had made if he still labors every day to make other things from nothing.[46] But they[47] respond that this text only refers to the creation of corporeal things, of which God is said to have made none after the first creation from nothing, since whatever corporeal things are created each day arise from the seeds of the first creation, and no corporeal thing may exist that does not descend from this first beginning.[48]

Therefore, God has rested from the first creation of bodies, since afterward one does not find that he has made any body from nothing. But one finds this written about incorporeal [beings]: "My Father continues to work in this fashion, and I am working (Jn. 5: 17)."[49] Therefore, the orthodox say that the human soul in no wise descends from a soul, but that new ones are made daily by God for new bodies. Whence it is written: "And it will return to the dust of the earth whence it came, and the spirit will return to God who gave it [life] (Eccl. 12: 7)."[50] Let it be noted how explicitly it is said that dust is from the earth but that God has given spirit. And again, "We have had wise fathers of our flesh, and we paid them due respect; how much more so should we submit to the father of spirits, and live (Hebrews 12: 9)?"

See here also how clearly it is shown that we have men as fathers of our flesh, and that God is the father of our spirits, so that the flesh alone comes from man, while the new spirit truly is given by God in a new flesh. According to the orthodox,[51] a very difficult question arises: surely if I have only the body from Adam, and the soul is not from Adam but from God alone, since sin is only in the soul and not in the body, then how am I said to have sinned in Adam?[52] Adam sinned, and the sin was in his soul alone, and not in the body. However I do not receive my soul—in which sin is[53]—from him. How, then, am I said to have sinned in him? Because my body was in him when he sinned,[54] I would rightly be said to have sinned in him if sin were in the body. However, since sin is in the soul alone, how am I said to have sinned when he sinned if my soul was not in him at all?[55]

On genera, species, and individuals

The orthodox respond in the following way to this question, and say that they view the relation of individuals to species as different than species to genera, for species have substantially more than genera. The genus does not suffice to constitute the substance of the species, because with respect to substance the species has a difference beyond the genus, and from the standpoint of substance the species is more than the genus.[56] For man is more than animal, because man is rational, and animal is not rational.

Individuals have nothing more than the species from the standpoint of substance, however, nor with respect to substance are they any different than the species. For with respect to substance, Peter is nothing else but a man.[57] That there are several individuals under one species, however, does not make man something substantial; [individuals] are rather accidental [to the species].[58] For that reason, a single individual can be under a species, although a single species cannot be under a genus. As a result, if all human individuals but Peter are destroyed, the species man has a single individual, Peter. He is an individual on account of a collection of accidents, just as man is a species because it can be common to many individuals. The bird "phoenix" is a species because it can be common to many individuals, although it has only one individual. Phoenix is one thing; *this* phoenix is something else. Phoenix is a specific nature[59] which can be common: *this* phoenix is a nature, however, which is only individual. It cannot be anything other than singular. A phoenix is defined by genus and differentia, but *this* phoenix is discernible by the peculiarity of its accidents. "Individual" can not be said except of one. A species, even if it is said of one alone, can be said of many. Moreover, the species—even if it is said only of one—is universal;[60] the individual is only singular.

Reason apprehends the species from the genus and differentia, while sense knows an individual only from the peculiarities of its accidents.[61] The interior reason of the rational faculty is able to reach universals; the external cognition of the sensitive faculty is able to reach individuals. We sense individuals through the body; we perceive universals by reason. And when a species is predicated of a single individual, only then can one speak of the accident of the species and of the individual, although principally and in the first place accidents are in individuals.

That in each case the individual must be distinguished from the species

Therefore, when man was first made, the human soul was first made in one individual and then divided into another.[62] The nature of that human soul was whole and complete in two persons; "whole," I say, because it was never outside them;[63] "complete," because there was nothing of the human soul lacking to either person. But listen and distinguish these three. There was a human soul; there was Adam's soul; and there was Eve's soul. These three are distinct: the soul of Adam is individual, or if you prefer, a singular or a person, which is predicated of no one else. Likewise, Eve's soul is an individual, or person,[64] or singular, which is predicated of no one else. The human soul is a specific nature, not individual but common, which is predicated of two persons and is divided in them. Distinguish these three, and do not use only sense in distinguishing them but also reason, for it is not by sense but by reason alone that the individual is distinguished from the species. But so that this can be grasped more easily, a few things must be said of the individual, or of the singular or the person.

On the individual

An individual is made an individual[65] by the peculiarity of its accidents, so that it is predicated of nothing else. Certainly, higher things[66] are predicated of individuals, but individuals are predicated of nothing else. If the species is not present in several individuals but has only one individual, it is predicated of the individual but the individual is predicated of nothing else, as "phoenix" is predicated of this bird,[67] and "world" predicated of this world, and "sun" predicated of this star. And, in this manner "individual" is said as a "universal," not as a "whole."

Now, the individual is both in the whole — since it is part of the whole — and the whole is divided in it.[68] Nevertheless, the individual cannot itself be divided on account of its smallness, like unity in number, a point in a line or time, a letter in a sentence, or an atom in a body. So both that which is last among universals and that which is least among wholes is called individual: the latter because it cannot be divided into lesser parts; the former because it cannot be predicated of lower things. The individual of the whole comprises but is not comprised; the individual of the universal divides and is not divided. The individual of the whole is first in the composition of the whole, and the individual of the universal is last in the division of the universal. The individual of the universal has the universal itself whole and perfect in it; the individual of the whole has in itself nothing from the whole beyond itself.

On the singular

Truly, that is called singular which is distinguished in some property from all other things. This distinction of each thing from all others occurs not only in individuals but also in universals. To be sure, even universals have their properties by which they are distinguished from others, if not by sense then by reason. Reason grasps the nature of universals by the power of its own intellectual acuity. It distinguishes one universal from another and from individuals, so that although universals may be common they have a certain singularity to their essence, just like individuals. Therefore every essence is singular, the individual essence just as much as the universal essence, namely having a singularity to its essence by which it is perceived singly apart from others. And thus every individual is singular. However, not every singular is individual, because an individual is that which is only predicated of nothing else. Every thing, however, is singular.

On person

A person is an individual of a rational nature, so that of all individuals those alone are called persons that do not lack reason.[69] Therefore, there is no person in universals[70] nor in those individuals which are not rational. Every person, then, is an individual; but not every individual is a person.[71] Thus, a person is to an individual as an individual is to a singular.

The grammarian divides person into three: to wit, first person, second, and third. It is the first person who speaks. The second, to whom the spoken word is addressed, is an individual capable of reason, in which case it is properly a person. There is a third person, about whom the spoken word speaks, and if this individual is rational, it is then properly called a person. But according to the grammarian a question arises concerning the case of the third person: whoever speaks of a third person refers to everything about which the spoken word speaks.[72] But how can something that is not a rational individual be a person? How can a picture be said to be a person by virtue of being a likeness, when it is not a man? and how are those, as is customary in theatrical usage, said to be persons by virtue of some similarity when they are not properly persons?[73] Thus, what is lacking reason is said to be an individual, but it is not a third person. Reason, however, has the property of speech, so that only that which has reason has speech. The "personhood" of reason, then, is divided according to the diverse modes of speech, so that the first person is the one who fashions speech; the second the one to whom we speak; and the third the one about whom we speak.[74]

Having distinguished persons according to these three modes of speech, the third [mode] of the three persons applies to all things through a certain analogy.[75] For just as speech (*locutio*) applies only to a rational individual, so too a term (*sermo*) can be formed for all other things. Indeed, it is correct and fitting for rational beings to associate with their own kind and to retain their property [viz. speech] for their own genus, which, if transferred to another genus, would seem to be an alienation [of that property].[76] But since it is necessary for rational beings sometimes to pass beyond their genus and fashion a term for unrelated things, we call the unrelated things third persons even if they are not, because there is a strong likeness in them to the third person, to the extent that there is a term for these unrelated things. There are then some things that are third persons through a likeness, some that are truly rational beings through a property, since the faculty of speech pertains properly only to rational individuals. Now let us return to our subject.

That there are many goods for the soul

In the beginning when God created the human soul, he conferred upon it many goods. He gave it reason, by which it could distinguish the Creator from the creature. He gave it a will and freedom of the will, so that it would will what it wills from freedom and not from necessity. The soul must not be compelled to blessedness, to which there is no access except by justice, freely willed. He adorned it with justice, by which it could earn beatitude. And he submitted it to a free will so that it would be justly free and not of necessity. He made it indebted to justice, so that one who receives justice also would owe justice, and would be held guilty by a debt to justice if it forsakes by its will what it always ought to possess.[77] And because man was made to attain the heavenly city,[78] the power of propagating the body was given to the human soul, so that it would be able to generate a body from its body for another soul, through the cooperation of a man and a woman.[79] Consider the human soul at the beginning of its creation, endowed with so many goods, confined to two persons, never extended beyond them.

That in the person's sin is the nature's sin

Notice that both persons [namely, Adam and Eve] sinned by the suggestion of the serpent. Each one sinned, I say, while as yet their substance was nowhere else than in these two who possessed it, and it was not yet anywhere else but there. If truly a person sinned, he did not sin without his substance. It is then the substance of the person that is vitiated by sin, and sin infects the substance, which exists nowhere outside the sinful person. Now one and the same substance is both common and specific to each person. Therefore, in each sinful person, the specific nature — which is nowhere but in them — is infected by sin. Therefore the whole nature of the human soul is infected by sin in Adam's soul and in Eve's soul, who have sinned personally. That nature is a common substance and it is specific to each. To be sure, it is not yet the case that it is outside these two. If it had been divided among others, the whole would not have been corrupted on account of these two alone, because if these two had sinned perhaps some others would not have sinned. In *them* the nature of the human soul would be saved. Now then where could there be a sinless human soul when everywhere it was a sinner?

How human nature sins not through itself, but through a person

Perhaps someone will say: if the common nature, namely the human soul, sinned in these persons, who can deny that the species has sinned? But it is absurd to say this of the species itself, or to ascribe to universals what concerns persons alone. Besides, universals always are what they are and, howsoever individuals may be changed, universals endure immutably. And although the mutability of individuals may be predicated of universals, still it is not in them. We do not say that the species has sinned in itself, but only in persons. And although the accidents of individuals are predicated of universals, still they are not what they are in the universals themselves, but they are there rather in a secondary sense, and from individuals. For just as species are different from individuals, so too are their properties. As a result, that property of man which is a species, universal, common, an essence unchangeable in itself that is predicated of many, and other things by which universals are distinguished from universals, does not pertain to individuals themselves. Likewise, that Peter is an individual, a person, predicated of nothing else, changeable, and [all] the other things by which individuals are separated from universals — these do not pertain to universals.[80]

Concerning the properties of species and individuals

And because the occasion has been provided and it is useful to our purpose, it must be observed that properties of universals which are common to the universals themselves do not in any way pertain to individuals, just as those [properties] of the individuals which individuals have in common cannot be joined to universals, like those we described above.

These properties of universals, by which each one is separated from all others, are principally and in the first place in the universals themselves; in the second place they are applied to lower things, even as far as individuals. Similarly, those properties of individuals, by which each one is distinguished from all others, are principally in individuals; but in a secondary sense they pertain to superior things, for example the property of body, which is corporeal substance, pertains to all lower things, but in the first place to "body." In like manner, properties by which Peter is separated from other individuals — as Andrew's brother, or first of the apostles — are principally in him, while universals receive them from him in the second instance.

So, the property of universals is double; in the same way, the property of individuals is double. There is one property of universals by which they differ from other universals; another, by which they differ from individuals. Likewise, the property of individuals: there are some properties by which they are distinguished from individuals, and others by which they are distinguished from universals. For although there is one and the same substance in individuals and in species, it is necessary that they have properties through which a difference may appear between them, as between "man" and "Peter": although they are one and the same substance, they have differences by which they differ from one another. The latter is the individual and the person, the former is the common and the specific nature: they are one according to substance, and diverse according to properties. Through that which they *have*, they are different; through that which they *are*, they are one.

The unity of substance makes those things which are different, one; the difference of properties makes those things that are one, different. And so the species does not have in an individual that which differs from the individual, but in and of itself and apart from the individual it has that which differs from the individual, as if it were not really in the individual. However, a species does not have a property by which it differs from universals except in the individual, and thus it has it in the individual as if it were nothing else but the individual, although nevertheless the species is not the individual.

Likewise, the individual does not attribute to its species that by which it differs from the species. But certainly it possesses in itself and separately from the species that by which it differs from the species, as if it had nothing from the species, although really it has one and the same substance with the species. As an individual, however, it does not have that by which it differs from individuals except with the species. And so it has that with the species, as if it were nothing else but the species itself.

That because of the person's sin the nature's sin is in the soul

Since we speak according to the authority of Scripture, which treats the two persons at the first creation as one and calls them by one and the same name — that is, Adam — if the soul of Adam has sinned, then the human soul has sinned.[81] Therefore, the nature of the person, which is specific but can be common, sinned. But of itself and separate from the individual nature it has not sinned, for sin is not from those properties by which the species differs from the individual:[82] the person has sinned in and through the individual itself, which has no other substance than the human soul, because sin is of those properties by which the individual itself differs from individuals.

Accordingly, a person does not have sin in separation from his species, with which he has one and the same substantial being. There is in the first man a sin of nature personally, not naturally. Because principally sin is in the person who has sinned, and secondarily in the species which has sinned — but not as such [i.e., as species] — a person could not sin without being a substance, nor could a person[83] have sin except in a substance. However a person has sin; and so the whole substance has it. Whole, because it was not anywhere else but there; whole, because it had not yet been divided among other persons. Indeed, we say "whole" properly, and not rather "every."

What is the difference between "whole" and "every"

Now "whole" is said on account of its parts; "every" is said on account of individuals. "Every" is appropriate to universals; "whole" is fitting for composites. "Every" gathers together individuals, "whole" gathers together parts. Species, however, is not a collection of parts, but gathers individuals. And a composite is found only in individuals, so that they may be called whole. All universals are of a simple and incomposite nature, although sometimes they are said to be composed[84] by a certain analogy, as a species is composed of genus and differentia, in a manner analogous to [the composition of] matter and form.

That the human nature is unable to pass over to other persons without sin

And since the whole human soul in Adam is guilty of sin, it cannot be passed on to other persons[85] without sin. Neither can the human soul be made without the vice of sin. Everywhere it carries within itself a vice that, from the beginning, has stiffened in it. Every soul created after Adam, then, carries from its natural beginning something that in it is culpable. For the rest, if it were without sin it would not be a human soul, nor would it be of a sinful nature if it were not itself a sinner. Or, if one should say that it is not sinful, then it is necessary to claim that it is not a human soul. Whatever is shown to be a human soul is not created in this life without sin.

How Christ came without sin

What then do we say of the soul of Christ, which is human and without sin? It was said earlier that the power of propagation is given to the human soul so that it can propagate a human body from a human body by the cooperation of man and woman.[86] By the authority of divine justice and a necessity of nature it was required that, whatever kind of soul was to be created for whatever kind of body, just that kind of soul would follow in such a body, so that whatever the origin and source of its root is, just that kind of a human birth follows by a just necessity. That which comes from the propagation of man and woman is not different from its source. Since Christ did not come from a marital union and was made in the Virgin from the holy Virgin, not from a conjugal act but by divine power alone, he properly lacked sin.[87] Nor should one look for sin where there is only a divine work. More, he can rightly be without sin who was made apart from human action, so that one who was not made through men would not share sin with men.[88]

The soul of Adam has joined guilt to the gift of propagation, and to the good of propagation which God gave he has added sin which he did himself.[89] Those things which were joined in the beginning cannot be separated in posterity. For that reason, men who are born by human propagation carry sin by nature. You will be born by human propagation, so guilt follows of necessity. Accordingly, he whom human propagation did not produce can be without sin. Remove human propagation, and where will you find guilt? And on that account, Christ did not have guilt, because he did not have a human generation. Nor is human nature subject to sin except where there is human generation. Now, where there is only a divine operation in propagation there is no guilt, unless you blame God. Therefore, Christ would have been born without sin even if he were not God.

Why was there punishment for Christ who was without sin

Perhaps it is asked: Why did Christ — who did not sin — bear so much? He sustained our weakness, and weakness is that on account of which power can be exercised, not by necessity but freely and from compassion for men. Now, when he exercised powers in weakness even unto death, he provided an example of patience so that we would not fail in our weakness, but would endure adversities with patience, because "strength is made perfect in weakness (2 Cor. 12: 9)." Now what difficulty did pressures present to him, when the signs of his latent powers were being expressed?[90]

Who says it is useless for the grapes to be pressed by the winepress when he sees the pure wine distilled? Who does not vigorously grind the grain if he wants to find its hidden power? Thus in Christ our weakness was obvious outwardly and, by his contrition,[91] it might be clear how steadfast he was inwardly. Thus, without any sin of his own he deigned to suffer punishment for our sin, not only for that which we do but even for that with which we are born.[92]

What distinguishes natural and personal sin

There are two kinds of sin: natural and personal. Natural sin is that with which we are born and which we derive from Adam, in whom all men sinned. In him was my very soul, as species, not as a person or individual, but as a common nature. Now, the common nature of every human soul was corrupted with sin in Adam. And for that reason, every human soul is culpable according to its nature, even if not according to its person.

Hence the sin by which we have sinned in Adam is natural to me, while in Adam it is personal. It is heavier in Adam; lighter in me. For in him I have sinned not according to *who* I am, but *what* I am. It is not I who have sinned in him, but that which I am. As a man I have sinned, but not as Odo. I have sinned as a substance, but not as a person. But because the substance does not exist except in the person, the sin of the substance is the sin of the person, but not personal. A personal sin is what I do according to who I am, not what I am; by which I sin as Odo, not as man, and by which I sin as a person, not as a nature. Yet because a person is not without a nature, the sin of the person is also the sin of the nature, but not therefore natural.[93]

What is to come from the root

It can be objected that it has been shown[94] that every soul whatsoever comes from a root-stock, although orthodoxy has denied this. Now, every soul is created in a body [and] has no substantial being (*esse*) other than the specific being. But the first soul had a specific being. Therefore every soul whatsoever has a substantial essence from the first soul. Therefore, every soul comes from a root-stock which draws its substantial essence from the first soul.

But one may respond to this objection that they do not correctly understand root-stock who say that it is from the species. They do well not to ascribe to the species what belongs to the individual. For although the root-stock is unable to exist without the species, nevertheless the individual does not have a root-stock from the species.

The individual has its root-stock from an individual, but not according to the same species.[95] In fact, it comes from an individual of one species, through an individual of another species, into an individual of the same species which preceded it, so that the individuals at the two extremes are of the same species, but the middle is of another. The two extremes are of the same one, from which and into which the root-stock proceeds, but it is another species through which it proceeds. The middle is that through which; the extremes are those from which and into which — the first from which, and the last into which.

As a result, in an animal the first parent is that from which; the semen, the middle through which; the last, the progeny into which we say the root-stock proceeds. It proceeds then from the first, through the middle, into the last. First and last are of the same species, like man, under [the genus] animal. For if the parent is an animal and a man, the child also is an animal and a man. The semen is the middle[96] through which, yet it is neither animal nor man, but one of another species.

Even in plants, the first is that by which; the middle, the seed through which — that is, the seed itself; the last, that into which the root-stock of the plant goes. Therefore, the last plant comes from the first plant through the middle of the plant seed, which is not the plant.

One should not think that one coming after the first individual has a root-stock outside the species shared by each, unless it is through the middle, the seed. As often as a species is passed on from some individuals to a new one, we say there is no root-stock[97] there, unless it is through the middle, the seed. And, seeing that rational souls do not flow from a seed, the species is always passed on from the first soul to a new one without any root-stock. And if the new one receives the substance of the preceding soul, still there is no root-stock when no seed (*semen*) comes between them.

How it is that God does not sin when he creates a sinful soul

The materials summarized above prove that the human soul is created sinful in everyone, and that no one can create them but God, who creates all things. One must be anxious, then, lest God — who is the creator of the sinful soul — appear to be the author of sin.

But we say that, on the contrary, God is the creator of the sinful soul and is not the author of evil. Now, observe who first made the soul in the human race and who first committed sin and you will find that the soul is the work of God and that sin is the work of man. The work of God is good; the work of man is evil. When you say, "God creates the sinful soul," you say two things: the soul and sin. But refer each to its author, namely the soul to God and sin to man. Therefore, in the sinful soul which God creates[98] give to God his work and praise him, and give to man his work and blame him.

You say, "He creates the sinful soul." When you hear soul, it is God's; when you hear sin, it is man's. In this fashion God both creates the sinful soul and is not the author of sin. But, further, and in order to speak more clearly, let us substitute injustice for sin. "God creates the unjust soul." But God is blessed, because even in this he is just. For what is more just than to create the human soul unjust? Certainly, he had to create in me whatever was in the first man, because at birth one ought to have whatever the propagation of man and woman deserves. He creates, then, an unjust soul most justly, because he creates something just as it ought to be. If he were to create a just soul, he would be unjust, and act against himself. Now, he who had appointed that each future generation procreated in the human manner should follow its beginning, subverts that design if the future generation is born just,[99] separating the body from its head, so that the end would not be contiguous with its beginning. Then the human race would be a biform monster, having a head different from its body, and a beginning different from its end. See then that when you shrink from the notion that God creates unjust souls, you do not do something unjust yourself by flattering him foolishly and, when you think to honor him, you dishonor the most Just.

Besides, God gave justice to the soul, and for that reason it ought to have it, but the soul which ought to have justice freely abandoned it. So whose is the guilt when it lacks what it ought to have? The sin belongs to the one that freely abandoned justice; it is not God's, who did not force it. Nevertheless, it *ought* to have what it does not have. When therefore God makes the soul without the justice it ought to have, it is not God's fault but the soul's. But if he now makes the soul that freely abandoned justice without it, should he not be especially praised because he left it so many goods? Still the debt of justice and propagation remains to it, free will, and reason itself, by which it is superior to other animals.

Foolish soul, refrain[100] from testing the Creator and calling him unjust because he has not made you just. Let what you have suffice for you, because you have not deserved even that. Praise the kindness of the one who gives things undeserved; do not reproach the righteousness of one not giving unjust things. What if it does not please him to give the one being created all that you wish? Give thanks for the things granted, and pray to him for the others.

You wish to make him appear unjust so that you would appear just. But the immutable cannot be changed, nor can the Omnipotent one be compelled. He creates an unjust soul, but this is nothing else than to create something without justice, and not to give justice to one being created. If he does not wish to give more, accept what you have while giving thanks, and do not trouble him for other things except by praying. But perhaps you say: "I ought to have them." If you ought to have them, then show them. "I do not have them." You have had. "I lost them." Who took them away? "No one." How then have you lost them? "I sent them away freely." Then you will not be able to recover them except through some great act of recompense. Still other things ought to be said on behalf of the orthodox, but because we are tired, these must be reserved for someone else's treatise. **Here ends book two.**

Book III

That the whole man is said to sin through the soul, and not the body

The material summarized above holds that injustice does not have an essence, nor is it in the body, but only in the soul where justice ought to be; that souls do not come from a "root-stock" but from God alone, either from things already existing, or from nothing;[101] that every human soul, and the whole soul, has sinned in Adam; and, that after him there is no soul without sin except the soul of Christ, under the requirements of divine and natural justice.

Since, then, man's sin is not found in the body but in the soul, for that reason we have spoken up to this point of the soul. Man, however, regarding whom we have undertaken this entire discourse, consists of body and soul. He is not complete from merely one of the two without both,[102] although sometimes one is said to be a man based on merely one of the two, as a certain wise man places "man" under "body," descending from the most general to the last species, saying that man is an animated body, sensible, and rational — here substituting reason for speech, because just as the mind uses reason inwardly, the body uses speech outwardly. More, since often what belongs to the part is said of the whole, and what is said of the part cannot be denied to the whole, as a result in the same way that someone is said to be both a black body and a just soul so too every man, since he consists of a soul and a body, is said to be a sinner through his soul. Does the whole come from many parts? What belongs to one part is said of the whole,[103] nevertheless it is not said of every part. One is called a sinner who is possessed of a body, nevertheless sin does not pertain to the body.

That there is one person in several substances

Thus, Peter is called a person. Although "person" does not pertain to body, yet body is joined to soul so that together with the soul it has what it does not have per se. Therefore, an individual man is called a person not because of his body, but because of his soul. Now, the soul assumes the body in its person, with the result that there is a double substance in one person. This distinguishes the creature especially from the Creator, because the Creator has several persons in one substance, which utterly cannot be found in the creature.[104] The creature is discovered to have one person in several substances, which cannot be the case in the majesty of the Creator. The individual man, then, is of a multiple substance and one person: one person, multiple substance. The human person is composed of several [things], yet is not predicated of several. It is divisible, like a whole is divided through its members; it is indivisible, like a singular is undivided through its subjects. Because it has parts it is a whole; because it does not have a subject, it is individual.[105]

That in man there is a sin of nature on account of the person's sin

And just as something is said of the universal on behalf of the individual, so something is said of the whole on behalf of the part, so that an individual man, who has both a body and soul at the same time, is called a sinner on account of the soul alone. He who has at the same time a body and a soul is called a sinner on account of the soul alone. Sin does not pertain to the body, yet a sinner is one who has a body. Therefore one does not say that the soul alone has sinned in Adam, but that he has sinned through the soul, namely through one part as a whole composed of several parts.

Accordingly, one says that Adam has sinned because the soul which he had sinned. And if Adam sinned, man sinned, because if this man himself sinned, human nature, which is man, has sinned. In fact, at that time the whole human nature was in him, and nowhere else was there a human species.[106] When, therefore, the person sinned, namely the man himself, the whole nature sinned, namely the common nature of man.[107] And, in the person's sin the man of the common nature is made culpable.

Now, whatever Adam made of human nature in himself, that is what he handed down to those after him. And it is necessary that just what human nature has become on account of a sinner's foolishness must be passed on to his descendants on account of the Creator's justice,[108] so that what was said above concerning the part is[109] in the whole, and what was said concerning the soul is found in the whole man.

That no one can evade justice

This must be understood to apply not only for sin, but also for punishment. So, because God imposed punishment upon the first man on account of sin, punishment is passed on to his descendants with sin, and those who are created with sin are also born with punishment. Deservedly, he who did what he wanted contrary to justice suffers what he does not want on account of justice. Rightly, he unwillingly suffers punishment who willingly abandoned justice. Justly, he who willingly acted evilly is punished unwillingly, so that he who deserts justice does not escape justice. Now, if he deserts her by evildoing he meets her again while justly suffering.[110] If, disobedient, he abandons her, he returns to her when suffering severely. If he does not wish to be subject to justice in obedience, he is subject to her — willy nilly — in suffering. That very justice which he avoids with his will, he incurs by necessity. A just necessity compels him whom an unjust will enslaves.

That the merit of a rational nature resides in the will alone

Truly, we sin or act rightly in the will, because our whole merit is in the will. If indeed we merit something, we merit it by the will, and where the will is lacking there is no merit. Where there is merit, there is just punishment or reward.

Blessed is the God who has placed in our will whatsoever our future is to be. How, then? As we will, so shall we receive. If we will justice, the merit of the palm wreath follows according to our will.[111] If we will injustice, a deserved punishment follows against our will. Whatsoever we achieve is in our power because it is in our will. Now, nothing is in our power more than our will.[112] For those things which are in our power, the more they are in our power, the more they are in the will. And because our will is nearer to our power and is in it more than other things, for that reason it is *especially* in our power. Now, my power does not extend to what does not depend upon my will, for surely what is not in my will compels by necessity more than it allures by power. In all things, then, "The Lord is righteous and there is no iniquity in him (Ps. 91: 16 Vulg.)." Whatever we might will, he himself is good. For instance, if there is justice in love, rightly the Pious One will repay the will's reward; if something else is in love contrary to justice, rightly the Just One repays the will's punishments.

That a rational nature is punished according to what it chooses

And because a man is punished against his will, he is punished for what he loves, so that on account of the pain he may regret what he loves. Therefore he is punished in himself and in his own choices, because he loves himself and them. He is punished in himself, namely in soul and body. In the soul and the body man immediately suffered consequences by which he is punished for sin, which he had not had earlier because he had not deserved them. For instance, in the soul he is confounded by ignorance, consumed by fear, saddened[113] by sickness, tormented by its distress, and distracted by the innumerable cares of the body. In the body, wretched man is ceaselessly tormented by a heaviness, by the pains accompanying illnesses, by work's fatigue, the failure of our labors, the imbalance between feast and famine, the shivering rigor of cold, the wilting heat of summer, and by other imbalances beyond number, even in the end unto death. He is punished by the death of relatives, by the various misfortunes of friends, and by the misfortunes befalling their affairs.

That there can be no sin without punishment

These are the evils that God makes so that man will suffer for the evil that God did not make, but man did.[114] By these evils God made, humankind is justly punished for the evils that God did not make, but humankind did. The human race joins the evil which God made to the evil that God did not make,[115] so that wretched man might always have his punishment conjoined to his sin; so that he who lives this earthly life with sin might endure this earthly life with punishment; and, so that punishment might always weary the one whom sin enslaves. This is the miserable condition of humankind, this its inevitable necessity: that since we always have sin we always have punishment as well. In this life we cannot loose the neck from the yoke of sin, nor really avoid the necessity of punishment. This sin, and sin's punishment, was in the first man: the punishment from God, the sin from man.

Man's sin is an act against God; punishment is an act of God against man. And just as sin passed from Adam to all men, so too also the punishment for sin, for there could not be sin without punishment among men. It is necessary for God's vengeance to be against us for our sin, just as God's vengeance came upon the first man for his sin, so that those who contract this sin also contract the punishment.[116] We have inherited human nature as it was in the first man later [namely, after the fall], not as it was in him earlier [before the fall]. Human nature demands from us[117] what was in the first man later, not what was in him earlier. Because he lost what he had earlier, what he was later has remained. What was good earlier he lost; what was evil later has remained. Humanity cannot be propagated except as it was. For the same reason we are not but what it was. And, on that account, we are wretched because it was wretched.

That the soul of a man cannot be made unless of a human nature

One might ask: How are human souls created each day by God? Now, if the substance of a new person is the same as the species, how is it said to be new when its substance is old? How is it created now, when its substance existed from the beginning? Surely, the specific nature endures when a new soul is created for the nature. How then is it made new today when its nature remained in the species? It happens now *and* it [already] was? How is this?

Certainly there is an answer to this question. It is clear, according to the Catholic faith, that a new soul is created in a human body. A soul, moreover, comes to be which is created either from human nature, or a nature other than the human, or no nature. But it is impossible for a person to come to be out of no nature, or to be created between natures, because then it would have no nature. If, however, the soul is created in a human body of a nature other than the human — this is absurd even to suggest! It remains then that when a new soul is created it comes to be from a human nature. And so one concludes that a new [soul] comes to be from a nature which is not new. Therefore, God makes a new soul which does not have a new nature.

The same nature is, then, new and not new. In the person it is new, in the species it is not new. It is new by its personal property, but not new by its common property. Either a new soul is created by God from preexistents or a new soul is created, with respect to the person, from nothing of the same nature as Adam was, with respect to the universal.

When you say a person having a human soul is created, you do not say that the human soul [as common] was created but rather the human person. However, the person having a human soul is the individual soul. Therefore, it is not the human soul [as common] that is created, but the individual soul. The individual soul is created because earlier it was not. The human soul [as common] is not created because it existed earlier and was in other persons. Still, the individual soul is a human soul, and the individual soul is substantially what the human is. This individual and the human are of one and the same substance — that is, now created — remaining individual and specific, singular and common from the beginning. For that reason there is one and the same substance in both since, when the individual soul is created, it comes to be of a human nature: now made from nothing, it receives into itself what is made from the beginning.

The individual receives, I say, the common nature, so that it shares the same substance with it. And although they differ according to their properties, in their substance they are really the same. Certainly, new individuals are created daily[118] for the human soul, which become precisely what the human soul is substantially. A new individual is created "of the human soul," which of necessity is of the same nature, because it is impossible for an individual "of a human soul" to be created in a human body of a nature other than the human.

Furthermore, it can also be said that new souls are created, not in terms of what they are, but in terms of what they have; that is, according to property but not substance. So a new property but not a new substance comes to be, with the result that with the generation of a new property one can speak of the creation of an old substance. On that account an old substance is called new, because it is formed with a new property. And although no person may exist without a substance, nevertheless not substance but a property of substance makes a person, and for that reason a soul is said to be new on account of a new property. God gives a new property to an existing soul, and makes a new person; the species subsists, a property is given by God, and a new person is made. A property accrues to the common nature and, through the property, what was common becomes individual. Clearly, the property alone comes to be, not the nature; the property alone, not the substance, and yet the substance is said to be created through the property, so that a new soul is made for which there is a new property.[119]

We do not prefer this explanation to the previous one,[120] because we hardly dare say that God does not create substance but only a property in the creation of souls, lest we seem to denigrate from the perfection of omnipotence if he is said[121] to create accidents alone in persons and not substances. Still, we would allow the reader to hold whatever view he will. According to the orthodox, these arguments show that all men contract sin at their origin[122] and that all have sinned in Adam, although souls do not come from a common root-stock.

Concerning the material whole

Now it is necessary to address those who say that [individual] souls also have come from Adam, and thus all have sinned in Adam. But here we must first speak of the part and of the whole, just as earlier was done for the universal and the individual. Now, just as one was able to speak above the universal and the individual for the purpose of illustration, likewise it will be useful here to speak of the parts and the whole for the purpose of understanding.

"Whole" is said in many ways.[123] In one way it means what is integral, as naturally constituted by a composite of parts where the composite is like a form and the parts like matter. In fact, composition[124] accruing to the parts constitutes the whole. Without composition the parts create nothing. While in man the parts are the body and the soul, in the human body the parts are all its members: the former constitute the man, and the latter the human body. And just as the whole is constructed of parts, so too it is destroyed by the dissolution of the parts.

In many cases, it happens that the whole is of one genus, and the part of another, so that the human body of man falls under "body," and the human soul under "soul," but the whole man falls under neither, but rather under that which consists of both.[125] In this whole, neither the whole is predicated of the parts, nor the parts of the whole.

Such a whole of the species is always the individual. In fact, such a whole is not found in universals. Universals are what they are through themselves (per se), and are of an incomposite and simple nature. If they are said to be wholes, they are said to be such in their individuals, not through themselves.[126] Even the genera and species of quantity, which seem to indicate[127] nothing other than such wholes [constituted] from parts, have their parts and are wholes in individuals.[128] But they neither have parts per se nor are they wholes per se; rather, they are absolutes of a simple nature. Like the genera and species of numbers,[129] whose complete rational nature a consideration of parts comprehends, they do not have parts nor are they wholes per se; everywhere they are wholes through a composition of parts in individuals.

Still, philosophical reflection confers a composition upon universals, not in a proper sense, but one analogous to matter and form. For instance, they say that a species consists of genus and differentia,[130] just as if from matter and form. But the simplicity of nature is not lost in this composition of universals, just as parts do not make the whole's quantity, but an advening quality informs the "matter" in a simple manner.[131] In fact, there is no figure,[132] nor a composition of many into one, but a simple idea informing matter; nor does quality make any quantity informing a material subject, just like number according to the composition of material parts. Now the number of material parts posits quantity, since indeed number is a quantity.[133] The figure of a material subject posits quality, since indeed figure is a quality. Quality, however, does not pertain to a whole [constituted] of material parts, but quantity does on account of their number. Certainly, because universals do not admit a number of material parts, the whole of quantity does not pertain to them. So they are called composites in their composition, but they are of a simple and incomposite nature, always remaining what they are and immutable per se.

Concerning the formal whole

In another sense, a "whole" is said formally, because it is constituted from form and matter. Now, in one way the body of Peter consists of a human form and the matter of bodily mass; in another way, it consists of its several members and composition. Form is in the mass and the formal whole is constituted. This whole is not constituted by quantity, because one is not concerned with the multitude of material parts here, but only mass and informing form. Nor should it be called quantity (*quantum*) but rather quality (*quale*), because it is formal. In fact, it is a form and a quality. And it must be acknowledged that this whole is not found except in individuals of the species. Species do not have this composition, but only one analogous to it.

On the virtual whole

There is a "whole" which can be called virtual, because it arises from powers,[134] and it is found especially in individuals having souls: for the soul has certain powers and certain virtues of which it consists. It does many things by its own power, so that souls move their bodies in numerous ways according to the powers of the soul. Whence a human soul has a rational power, which it uses inwardly for the cognition of unseen things[135] and for the judging of all things, and it effects many acts outwardly in its own body, especially speech.

The name "sensible" is also attributed to the soul, whereby the body is endowed with the five senses so that it is able to perceive sensible things. More, it divides the different senses[136] among the parts of the body, according to the diverse qualities of sensibles; the eyes' vision apprehends shapes and colors; the ears' hearing perceives sounds and words; the nostrils, odor by smell; the palate judges flavors by taste; touch discerns everywhere throughout the whole body — the rough from the smooth, the hard from the soft, the thick from the thin, cold, heat, and shapes. Although these senses in the body are from the soul, still they are *not* the soul, nor even the power of the soul, but affections carried from the soul into bodies.

Furthermore, the soul has a nutritive[137] power by which it nourishes its body and even regulates, without being aware of them, the changes of its body's states. What can we say of the souls of plants? Certainly, medical science does not ignore their internal powers, and explores the virtues of these plants according to diverse species.[138] Internally, they have a soul's powers, and externally the plants are influenced. The soul's power moves, and this is found in plants. We experience in plants the powers that are latent in the soul. It is remarkable that, with the soul dead, the powers of the soul remain in the body and the vestiges of powers that were in the soul remain in plants, until at length these pass away little by little in the body with age.[139] However, the soul has this peculiar property such that even though it has several powers, it is wholly in each; and the soul is in individual powers, although nevertheless the whole does not consist of a single power.[140] The whole is in one power alone but one power alone does not cause the whole; there is indeed a whole in individual powers alone, yet it does not consist of individual powers alone. The whole is predicated of a single part, but the whole does not consist of a single part. And although the soul of this plant may be predicated of its separate powers, nevertheless their species is not considered, since it is individual and is predicated of no subject. The powers of this soul *are* its parts, *not* like individuals to a subject; nor is the soul of this plant whole in its individual powers, although the whole species is in its separate individuals. Now let us return to our undertaking.

How souls come from a "root-stock"

Those who defend the propagation of souls, whose account we have employed in an orthodox manner, say that every soul comes from a root-stock: that is, a soul comes from a soul through a seed (*semen*), just as its body is propagated by its seed from a body, or a tree from a tree. Thus, [they say that] the seed power is in the soul, just as in the body.

In animals, unless the seed of the parent draws off a nutritive power, it does not lead to the creation of a next offspring. For instance, how does a seed that is introduced to a female grow if it does not draw upon the nutritive power of the soul? How will a seed inseminated in the womb of a pregnant woman grow, unless it has been animated in some way? Let the urine, or fluid, or some other thing flow[141] from the parent, it still does not result in a birth or in a child, nor is an animal ever born by such an infusion because this infusion is lacking animation. Such an infusion draws no power from the soul, and on that account produces no birth, nor does anything grow from it.

Let a seed be introduced to a woman, and let another fluid be introduced. How is it that the latter is always useless, while the former often grows into a child? the latter never avails anything, while the former promises a child in the future? How is this so, unless the latter is not animated at all while the former truly possesses a nutritive power? Therefore, the body's seed draws with itself the seed of the soul, namely the power of growth, which power nourishes the corporeal seed into a human form, the power growing with it into a rational soul. As a result, just as a particle which is not a human body flows from the human body in sowing the seed, so a particle which is not a human soul flows from a human soul like the seed. And just as it is not customary for a body's lust to arise without the soul's delight, so too lust does not produce a seminal fluid from the body unless at the same time the soul's delight should produce a seed's power from the soul: that is, a nutritive power, so that it might become the seed of the human soul; a nutritive power [is the seed of the soul], just as the seminal fluid is the seed of the body. Just as the causes proceed at the same time, namely delight and lust, so too the effects follow at the same time: that is, a nutritive power and a seminal fluid. Moreover, they grow at the same time with the one growing—the latter into a human form, the former into a rational soul. From then on they remain together in one person unto death. The conjoined causes join their effects simultaneously into one individual, which consists of body and soul. That individual, however, composed under its species through its causes, grows into an individual of another species. In order to see that more clearly let us begin again, so that an understanding of the conclusion may become plainer from a higher starting point.

The descent of substance to the individual, through that which arises from body and soul

There is a genus subordinate to substance which is not placed beneath body or soul, but beneath that which consists of both. And this one has another subordinate to it: that is, it consists of the nutritive soul and body, having animal opposite it. However, that which consists of body and the nutritive soul itself has another *suppositum*, another subaltern: that is, an animal seed, which is not an animal, but only the seed of an animal having plant opposite it. As a result, that which consists of a body and a nutritive soul is a plant, on the one hand and, on the other, the animal seed. Under animal seed man's seed is the most specific species, and thence comes the individual seed of each man. Man's seed, however, under animal seed, is neither a man nor an animal but gradually grows into an individual man.

The animal seed, which is not an animal, flows down and gradually grows into another individual animal. And in this way an animal is propagated by an animal, through an animal seed, which is not an animal. As a result, the animal seed, losing the specific nature of a seed which it had, receives the substance of another species by a sort of growth, which [substance] it possesses thereafter.

Illustrating the Descent of Substance into the Seed of the Individual Human
(Source: (D) fol. 108ʳ, (B), and (M) col. 1095)

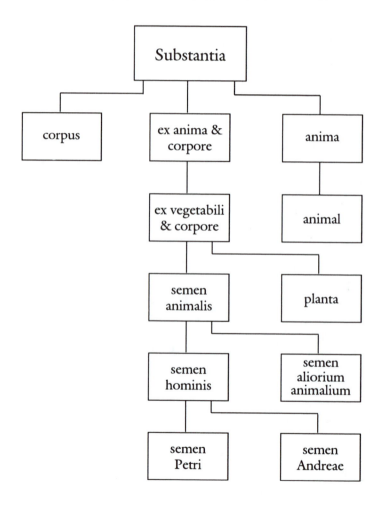

That species and individuals are changed in the same matter

In this it must be noted that a change of species and individuals occurs in the same matter, and in the same mass at one time one species arises and at another time another[142] arises, so that in the seed's mass there is now a seminal nature, later a human nature. And although the mass is the same materially, temporarily it changes its substance according to predication. As a result, while the same lump of matter remains, just as sometimes the shape[143] is changed in it, so too the specific nature and even the individual is changed, because the individual follows from the species and not its matter.

To be sure, the individual is not concerned for the material subject below, but for the form-bearing species above. Thus, it frequently becomes clear in bodies, as in corporeal mass, that just as the shape is changed with respect to matter the species is changed according to predication. The shape fashions the mass and it becomes a formal whole corporeally; the differentia forms the substance, and it becomes a substantial species incorporeally. When the form is changed, the matter is visibly changed in individual things; when the differentia of the common substance is changed in the visible matter, the specific nature is changed in the same visible matter invisibly, so that a change of the corporeal shape in the mass can be said to be caused by an incorporeal change of the differentia in the substance.[144] Just as bodies change their shapes, so that from their materials they become different formal wholes, so too the genera of bodies change differentiae in the materials of bodies, so that other species arise; there shape (*figura*) forms the matter from the differentiae themselves, with the result that the matter itself consists of material parts. The differentia forms the genus, with the result that the species is predicated of individuals in matter itself. From the one you have the parts of matter; from the other, you have the substance, and the matter itself is placed in between. Because matter has parts it also has substance.

Substance is predicated of matter; matter is composed of parts. From the one matter receives the predicate substance, and from the other it has a composition of parts. From the one it is an individual, a specific substance, and from the other it is a whole from its parts,[145] since as an individual it is referred to a species, as a whole it is concerned with parts. Though related to both, the individual comes after each. For instance, it is posterior to the species as an individual, and posterior to its parts as a whole.[146]

That every complete whole is the middle term of extreme principles

Every complete whole, then, stands in the middle between its parts and its predicates. It contains parts from below; it receives predicates from above. From above it receives its substance, from below its wholeness. From its predicates it has the highest principle it may be; from its parts the lowest principle from which it comes. From the predicates following its highest principle it receives the differentiae of species, descending to it gradually; from its parts, on the side of its lowest principle, it receives a composition of parts, gradually ascending to it. One and the same thing receives predication from its predicates, and from its parts it accepts composition. One and the same thing is both whole and individual. It is individual because it *is* something; it is a whole because it is *from* something.

It is individual because higher ones are said of it; it is a whole because lower ones comprise it. It is individual because it is not said of a subject; it is whole, because it is composed of many. Composition does not pertain to the individual nor predication to the whole, because a whole is not said to receive a predicate nor an individual to admit composition. Every integral whole, therefore, which is capable of receiving some figure (*figura*), has two principles: the highest for this [predication] and the lowest for that [composition]. The lowest is related to the highest, because it is its individual; the highest is related to the lowest, because it is its whole. The lowest is related to the highest, because it is not said of a subject; the highest to the lowest, because its end is established from it. It is lowest, because it descends by its predicates until it is said of nothing lower; it is highest because it ascends from its parts until it proceeds no further. It [the integral whole] reveals itself to be the middle term[147] of each principle, so that the function of each terminates in it. Now, the term of predication comes from the highest principle, and the term of composition from the lowest. And in it the terms of the two extremes come together at the same time, so that returning to the same place it finds a term from the one and the other. So, something consisting of one hundred has [two] extremes: from the one, unity; from the other, quantity. At the bottom, it is an individual from quantity according to predication; at the top, a whole from unity according to its composition.

On highest and lowest principles

The extremes are, from above, principles of predication for individuals; from below, they are principles of composition for wholes.[148] The term for the principle of predicables is the individual; the term for the principle of parts is the whole.

The first principles enclose the universe of their objects from both sides by their extremity. Because they leave nothing outside [that universe] things being propagated (*propagationes*) from them turn inward toward one another to the same thing, so that the same thing according to diverse relationships is the middle boundary[149] of each process. The lowest are not placed beneath the highest by predication; rather they look upon each other from opposite sides, and just as opposites, the highest are not predicated of the lowest, nor are they composed from these.

Nevertheless, the lowest extreme does not really reject the highest.[150] For instance, the point of a line, although it is not yet a line, nevertheless is not really not a line, but is almost a line. It is then a line in a certain fashion, although it is not a line in every sense. Similarly, a letter too is not fully a word (*vox*),[151] but almost. It is not a word in every sense, but in some measure; it is not a complete word, but an incomplete word. It is then a quantity in a certain fashion. Likewise, an atom of a body is almost a body, and the point of time is almost time, and unity almost number. Therefore atoms are substance in a certain fashion; these others are quantity in some fashion. The grammarian, who calls number singular as well as plural, studies this.[152] He, and common usage, call present time a particle of time, to which as a common term past and future are joined. And thus last principles can be referred to the first, just as when placed beneath genera they assume their predicate for themselves.

On figure

It can be inferred from the preceding that figure (*figura*) becomes the cause of all corporeal things; for without figure even matter cannot be, nor can any species be predicated of individuals in bodies, nor can a material whole be or be composed. Now although corporeal matter can be *conceived* in the mind, it cannot *exist* without figure.[153] Take away the figure which has just now been formed, and the species itself which is predicated perishes. For instance, if the figure of a human body perishes, the species itself departs from the body and the body[154] assumes another species according to some other figure which it has received. Now when it receives the figure of ashes or of a worm, it also changes the species in the same material mass.[155] And, what earlier was called a man with respect to some material mass, according to its prior figure, is now called a worm or ashes according to another figure with respect to the same material mass. Similarly, even the material whole cannot exist without the figure for its mass. For example, how are its parts distinguished if they are not fashioned in a material mass?[156] Indeed, figure is the cause of all bodies. To be sure, neither wholes nor individuals can exist, nor have a species, nor in any way subsist, without figure.

On forms

Similarly, no incorporeal things can exist without their forms, as all species and individuals receive differentiae and properties and forms, by which they exist. The first genera of things receive essence on behalf of form. Now, just as forms give being to their subjects,[157] so too the highest genera cannot exist except through essence. All other forms belong to their respective subjects, but essence is common and universal to all things. Other forms cause their subjects to be something: essence causes all things to be *simpliciter.* And since all things have proper forms by which they are formed to be something, the first genera of things have essence by which they are formed for existence.[158] Other forms make their subjects *what* they are; but essence makes every thing *that* it is.[159] And since it is one thing to be something, and another merely to be, some forms pertain to being something, and not simply to being. And although to be something follows from being, it does not belong to other forms to cause being. They cause things to exist not by nature, but consequent [upon existence].

However, essence is first among first genera, so that first genera exist in a principal sense, with the result that they receive the form of existence in the first place through essence. From there, lower genera are determinate being through their forms, as body has substantial being through corporeal form. Therefore, forms are the causes of all things. Certainly, all other forms are the cause by which their subjects are something determinate; essence, however, is the cause by which all things simply exist. Now, matter is prior to form in a substantial nature; but forms, if you have a view to being, are prior to matter, because they make it exist.

But we have digressed too often and too long in this work. The difficulty of our undertakings, which generates various questions, compels us to look at many.[160] These ought to be solved with clarity, lest what problems there are remain in obscurity. The subtlety of the questions, which can hardly be understood even with an extended discussion, pushes us further. Like the head of a living hydra, when we cut off one, many are regenerated, which cannot be removed without great effort.

That the nutritive power is the seed of the soul, although it is not the soul

Above it was shown that the animal seed belongs to those things which consist of body and soul, and also that just as the body grows in the seed so too the nutritive power grows into the future animal. According to this view, it cannot be denied that as a body is made from a body, thus even an animated soul is made from an animated soul through a nutritive soul.

Perhaps someone will say that since the power is in the nutritive seed there is no soul coming from the soul of the parent and growing into the soul of the progeny. But what was said above guards against this, affirming that soul is said of the individual parts just as of the whole.[161] But if perhaps some importunate person will not submit to this argument: so be it! One who has intelligence[162] cannot say that the nutritive power is not of the soul. And if, as he says, it is not a soul, still it is a power of soul. For unless a body has a soul insemination cannot proceed. Take away the soul, it does not make a seed. It makes a seed, therefore it has a soul. Seed has the nutritive power, then, from the soul. It has it either from the soul, or the body. If from the body, remove the soul and provide a seed and we will give you the palm of victory if we see some progeny result. If it cannot be done, confess the truth and concede the nutritive power to the soul.

Even if the power itself is not the soul, through it a soul is propagated by a soul, and the seed of the propagating soul becomes a soul. Whether that power is called a soul or not, it is clear that it comes forth from the soul of the parent, and grows into the soul of the progeny. Moreover, whatever [seed or fluid] is imparted from the parent—whether from one or the other—remains sterile and useless because it does not carry within itself the power of a soul.[163] Further, often we shall see a likeness of the parent in the progeny, both in the body's appearance and in the soul's habits. How is this possible, unless the seed draws from the body a little fluid and from the soul the nutritive power? Now, unless the seed would bestow upon each progeny what it draws from each parent, it would not represent in each of the progeny the complete likeness of the parents.

That we were all in Adam in soul and in body

If, then, there is found in the seed both what comes from the soul and the body, it is clear that the soul of the progeny comes from a "root-stock,"[164] and all our souls were in the soul of Adam. When Adam sinned, no aspect of human nature was absent in him, but the whole of whatever was man was still in him. So when he sinned, we all sinned, because we were all in him. We were in his body and we were in his soul. Therefore, in him we are all infected by sin, and because vengeance justly falls upon him on account of sin, so justly punishment with sin is visited upon us. And justly we are born wretched, we who come forth from misery, so that the conditions of our origin apply even to the succeeding generation.

So, we are born with sin, which is original for us, because it was a personal sin for the first man. We are born with a sin which we ourselves did not do, but which he did himself, and he transfers to us the misery which he has himself deserved. And this is the original sin in which humankind languishes, and from which Christ freed us.

Why God is called Father of Souls

By the authority of Scripture, the orthodox contend that a soul is not propagated by a soul. For Solomon said: "Let the dust return to the earth whence it came, and the spirit to God, who gave it (Eccles. 12: 7)."[165] And the apostle says: "We have had learned fathers in the flesh and revered them; how much more should we submit to the Father of spirits and live (Heb. 12: 9)?" Against this the propagators of souls[166] say that while God made the body of man from the earth, he made the soul from nothing. Although parents may beget both the soul and body in their progeny, nevertheless God is properly called the Father of the soul,[167] because man receives it nowhere else but from God alone, so that while he gets his body elsewhere, God is rightly said to be father of that which does not come from any other source. Because according to Scripture God is properly called father of the soul, it remains for man to be called father of the flesh, even though he may beget both.[168]

That souls do not come from a "root-stock"

The propagator of the soul argues that the soul comes from a soul for the reason that the nutritive power is carried in the seed, saying that the power itself is a part of the soul, and that it is separated from the whole in order to produce a child. The orthodox position says that this smacks of "carnality," and does not know well the nature of the soul. Surely the human soul is a simple and incomposite nature. It is not composed of several things, although it may consist of several. It is one, and has many powers, just as the sun is one, and has many rays. It is simple and conveys[169] many things from itself to the body. Outside of it they are many, but they come from that which is simple within itself. There are "parts" to the soul, but it has no composition, because the whole itself does not admit quantity.

Here the propagator of the soul errs, because when he hears "parts" he thinks "quantity," and he looks for an attribute of the body in what is not a body. Inasmuch as it is in a body he thinks that a part of the soul can lie hidden, and that its individual unity, which is not in a place, can be broken up into discrete places; and he thinks that the soul can be contained in several places by discrete parts, and have parts just like discrete places contain a body. He has a carnal understanding because he judges spiritual things after the manner of bodily things, since he seeks corporeal quantity in a spiritual substance. He hears "parts" and "quantity" occurs to his mind, and composition, which is wont to be of body; passing on from the soul to the body and thinking about it according to the body, the soul in itself was even forgotten. He seeks it outside itself, thinking that it is distended by quantity and expanded across spatial locations, even though it does not have number but is incomposite, as unity in number is much simpler than the point of a line, or the atom of a body, which, although it is of a body is not yet itself a body, but is incorporeal on account of its simplicity.

When then you hear "parts," remove any notion of quantity or composition in the soul from your mind and, purging it of the phantasms of bodies, put aside sense and imagination and raise yourself up to reason, so that you contemplate Reason with reason. To be sure, the parts of a rational soul are not bodies but potencies, not material things but efficient powers. They do not comprise it like members but come forth from it like rays [of the sun]. It is a whole; it is not extended by length. It is a whole; it is not diffused by breadth.[170] It is a whole; it is not enlarged by depth. While it consists of several things, it does not lose its simplicity because it admits no composition. It consists of several things, yet guards the individuality of its unity because plurality itself does not constitute quantity. Indeed it is true that the power of propagation in the seed comes from the soul,[171] but that power is an affect of the body not an efficient power of the soul. Efficient power is in the soul and the body is affected by its presence.

I say, consider and distinguish three things: the soul, the power of the soul, and the power of the body. The soul is substance. Moreover, the power of the soul is also called substance and soul. But the power of the body is not substance, nor soul, nor the power of soul. Rather, it is an affect of the body: that is, a quality conferred upon the body by the presence of the soul. Still, this quality can be called a power of the soul in some sense, not because it is a part of the soul, but because through the power of the soul it is conferred upon a subject.

The soul not only affects the body by its efficient powers, but also by its qualities, so that we often see that the face grows pale from fear or blushes from shame[172] in the soul. Many passions of the body occur from the efficient powers and qualities of the soul. Thus, the soul rules by its powers and qualities and changes the body. It itself remains whole in itself, while the body is affected by the many qualities of the soul, which themselves are not souls. So the soul exerts its powers throughout the entire body, although it is not itself the whole body. Rather, it infuses itself as a whole throughout all the extension of the body, yet has no extension. The body has parts, and the soul fills the body, yet not by its own parts, but whole and full and perfect[173] it fills the individual parts of the body. It fills several (*plura*), I say, without plurality; a great number, without number; many (*multa*), without multitude.

In like manner highest wisdom possesses all forms of all things. Many forms are discernible in the highest science,[174] since there are many things in creation, because diverse things are made in creation according to the diverse forms of highest science. In fact, highest science saw within itself how all things would be created outside of it. Thus all things have gone forth into an essence[175] in the way that eternal forms have directed.

Look, we say that there are many forms in the highest science, although not unless they are all one [science].[176] Whatever is there is but one, and that one, O one Light, has several rays. The rays are one in one light, yet they appear many in the manifold creation. There are many forms of one science, yet the science itself is one form.[177] Simple in itself, it appears manifold in creation.

But even created things receive their forms from the highest science, since they are conferred upon its objects by eternal forms. Temporal things are produced from eternal ones, lower from highest. Certainly, the forms of things do not come out of these [temporal objects], with the result that they are not of this but of another nature, because the one is the Creator, the other, creatures. Thus, they do not come forth from the highest so that the highest essence might flow down into creation bit by bit and bestow parts of its substance upon creation, as if our forms are that which the highest is; but the highest creates, and these arise from its efficient powers.[178] It fills the whole creation, yet is not a whole. It fills every space, yet has no extension; all times at once, without time; full and whole and perfect it fills the individual parts of the whole creation, without parts of its own.

Similarly, a soul fills its body because God made a soul in his likeness. Therefore the soul rules its body, and the body has many things by the soul's presence which are not of the substance of the soul, nor parts of substance, but affections and qualities of body. The body even has many things from the soul which it retains for some time after the soul has departed. For instance, a limb newly cut off from a living body[179] palpitates for a time after the soul has departed, retaining the motive power it had from the soul. And a cut herb,[180] after it has been dried out for a long time and reduced to finest dust, once it has lost the soul in every sense, nevertheless retains from the soul which was lost a sweet-smelling fragrance and powers against illnesses. In like manner, the seed produced from a living body by desire draws a power of propagation with it from the soul, the power it had in the body from the soul. Certainly, it was not of the soul, but of the body from the soul, namely a quality and *affect* of the body, but an *effect* of the soul. The seed is produced and separated from its body, and carries beyond itself the nutritive power which it had. The seed carries a power with itself beyond the body, but the body retains the soul within itself. Nothing is separated from the soul with the seed, but the whole soul remains in the body. The seed carries within itself the soul's influence, but the body retains its whole soul. Nothing can emanate from a simple nature. A soul then cannot produce from itself another soul. Nor can we find a "root-stock" from which you said a soul is made.

Why philosophical reasons are used in this work

I beg you, brothers, not to censure me[181] for the philosophical concerns which we raised, as if I wished to strengthen the Catholic faith through philosophical reason. I did not do so in order to strengthen it, but in order to teach. Who can strengthen truth? Truth cannot be made stronger, because it cannot be changed.[182] But truth is heavy and weighty; it is not a trifling thing (*levis*) for the unreliable senses (*levibus sensibus*), nor does the untutored quickly apprehend that which the learned man barely discovers. Therefore, reasons must be sought, not so that the strongest be strengthened, but so that the hidden be revealed; not so that the unchangeable be confirmed, but so that things that are cloaked with mysteries be disclosed. And for this reason we have employed certain philosophical arguments: because we learned from the clergy that Catholics, trained in the liberal arts, see hidden things more quickly through those things which they have already learned.

Why the propagators of souls are treated here

On that account, I freely brought forward the propagators of souls so that, after all the issues had been examined on all sides, the choice would appear more easily and, among the many options brought forward, the authority of truth would shine freely and the treatment of the opposed positions would appear a simple thing.[183]

Here ends the third book

A Disputation with the Jew, Leo, Concerning the Advent of Christ, the Son of God

Prologue. Odo, Bishop of Cambrai, to Acard, monk of Fémy:

When I was in the chapter of Fémy, just before the nativity of the Lord, I provided an explanation for the divine Incarnation. What you heard was pleasing, as you said then, but your memory was unable to retain what it had understood, for those explanations which remain after an economical presentation, with a more copious one fall away into confusion.[1] For that reason you asked for a concise argument summarized as if with a sharp point[2] in order to form your memory, which a flood of opinions was choking. Finally, overcome by your pleas, I proposed to do what you asked. But because on one day when I went to the council of Poitiers[3] I was pressed into a discussion against a certain Jew of Senlis[4] — quite fittingly, on this very matter (with the help of God) — so it seemed appropriate to me to pursue this question in the form of a dialogue, where the Jew had asked and I had responded. Because the Jew is named Leo, and I am called Odo, let each person be identified by the first letter of his name.[5] I call then upon the Holy Spirit so that what he gave to me once in order to convince the Jew he would now give me again in order to instruct a Christian monk. And so, when the Jew came to our lodging after siesta time, toward the ninth hour,[6] he began to speak to us as we were seated together.

That the remission of sins is not adequate for glory

Leo: Tell me, bishop, what benefit did the coming of your Christ confer upon the world?

Odo: Tell me, Jew, what benefit do you believe that your messiah will bring, whom you believe is yet to come?

Leo: Whatever we read in the prophets, namely that all kingdoms will be subjected to us through him; that we will have perpetual peace under him; that we shall be gathered from all the kingdoms into Jerusalem; that Jerusalem will have dominion over all kingdoms; and, all other things which the prophets happily enumerate. Since we do not see all these things fulfilled in your Christ, we wonder what you expect from him?

Odo: We expect the kingdom of heaven through Christ, and we await that felicity which you hope will be earthly, but which through Christ we hope will be heavenly.

Leo: You seem to err. We hope both for temporal happiness through the messiah and for a heavenly kingdom after this life through the observance of the law. The prophets promise us temporal goods, and we expect the kingdom of heaven on account of the law, for the law teaches what kind of sacrifice there is for each sin, and thereby sin is forgiven. For the prophet Nathan said even to King David, who confessed to the sin of adultery and homicide: "Your sin is forgiven (2 Kgs. 12: 13)." If there is forgiveness for sins in the law apart from Christ, then eternal beatitude also follows, "For men are blessed whose iniquities are forgiven and whose sins are covered over (Ps. 32: 1 Vulg.)." What, then, does your Christ do?

Odo: You do not pay sufficient attention to the requirement of justice. He whose sin is forgiven is not immediately promoted to glory. The remission of sins removes the punishment, but does not confer glory. Glory is not immediately given to him, whose punishment is removed. Although his anger has been forgiven, he is not clothed at once with grace. Even when David forgave his son for the crime of murdering his brother, he did not permit him to be brought before him immediately, nor did he bestow grace upon him whose wrath he had forgiven (cf. 2 Kgs: 13–14). Indeed, man has sinned in the same manner.[7] Punishment is dismissed under the law for the penitent, for one who is once again obedient, as well as for one serving well. But he still does not merit glory, to which justly he may not approach unless recompense for sin [has been made]. It is unjust to admit[8] a sinner among those who have not sinned, without satisfaction for the sin. Remission of sin, then, was given to man under the law. Yet because man is unable to offer satisfaction for sin under the law, he cannot approach to glory through the law. For that reason Christ is necessary to the world, because in him we offer satisfaction for sin in order to come to glory.

That the performance of good works does not suffice in order to remove sins

Leo: I do not know how man may offer satisfaction for sin through your Christ. I see, however, how sin is corrected under the law. For by petitions and sacrifices, oblations, alms, and other acts of good works, we offer satisfaction for sin to God under the law.

Odo: Suppose a servant is obligated to his lord for an old debt. If later on he sins again against his lord, how will his later sin be purged by payment of the old debt? Or will settlement of the older debt justly be counted as satisfaction for the later sin? Does not a just lord require something separately, first for the debt and then for the sin?

Leo: Yes, certainly.

Odo: Then man was not able to correct sin by doing good works. For every good which he had been able to do before sin he already owed to God, from whom he had received them. Even if a man should repay every good which he has received, nevertheless something [more] is justly demanded of him for the evil he has done. Man cannot, then, redeem the sin he has committed by any acts of holiness under the law.

That suffering misfortunes does not suffice in order to remove sin

Leo: If man was not able to redeem sin through that which he owed before, so be it. But surely he was not obliged to suffer hardships or death before; who, then, would say that he ought to suffer them, seeing that he had not deserved them? We read however that God imposed these penalties upon man for sin. "For on the day that you shall eat, you will die the death (Gen. 2: 17)." Thus, death. "In the sweat of your brow you will win your bread" and the earth "will grow thorns and thistles for you (Gen. 3: 17–18)." Thus, hardships and tribulations. If God has imposed these punishments upon man for sin, either they do or they do not suffice to expiate sin. If they suffice, it follows that once sin has been expiated we may approach heavenly glory, and without your Christ. If they do not suffice, it must be said that God has very wrongly enjoined penalties that do not suffice to expiate sin. But this is a wicked thing to say about God. Thus it is proved that God, being wise, has appointed[9] the measure of punishment according to the measure of sin. For a just God had to exact a just vengeance, which would not be less than the sin nor exceed it in measure. Being just, he ought not punish the sinner less than he deserves nor, being pious, more than he deserves. Therefore, if man patiently bears the hardships of this life, its tribulations and, at the end, death, he corrects sin by virtue of the suffering[10] which he did not owe earlier because one who had not sinned did not deserve to suffer.[11] Accordingly, sin is removed by the recompense of some good, because to the extent that the crime was evil, to the same extent good is restored by suffering. When sin is forgiven, therefore, what prevents one from entering the Kingdom [of glory]?

Odo: You would not say these things if you understood how weighty sin is. For that reason let us inquire into sin — the very least sin we can — in order to see thereby how heavy sin is in all other cases. Why don't you yourself propose whatever pleases you.

Leo: No sin appears lighter than a fleeting, vain thought.

Odo: Suppose that God enjoins you not to turn away from him even with a momentary lapse of thought, and someone else says to you that unless you turn your thoughts quickly toward another you will perish immediately and return to nothingness. Do you really think that for your own sake and in order not to perish you ought to turn your thoughts even briefly to another and against God, or that you should commit even such a trifling sin for your redemption? Or do you think that it is better for you to live by sin than perish for justice?[12]

Leo: Why not better?

Odo: Because God omnipotent can restore you, after having guarded justice, to a better condition than the one you seek to enjoy through sin. He who may justly make you wretched for living through sin, also may justly restore you, once you have died for justice, to a blessed state. That sin which you have proposed, then, weighs you down heavily; it is not one that you ought to commit even for your redemption.

Leo: What you say pleases me. I did not realize that such a little sin had so much significance.

Odo: But now tell me: should you do for an angel what you ought not to do for yourself?

Leo: According to the reason which you gave me, one ought not oppose God even in the least little thing for anyone, nor for everyone, nor for all creation. For God omnipotent is powerful enough to restore one who could have perished on behalf of justice to a better condition; and to those to whom he once mercifully gave existence and not according to merit, he may now justly and according to merit grant a better existence.

Odo: You have understood well. Now, no creature can remove that which in some other creature opposes God, lest God appear to need a creature to remove what is opposed to him in a creature. A slave cannot free a fellow slave. And since every creature is a servant of God, no created being[13] can free another creature, who submitted to sin, from sin. The one who submitted to sin withdrew from God; a creature that frees a creature from sin restores it to God and makes it blessed. But it is better to be blessed than merely to be. And so they would attribute to the creature what is greater and to God what is less, if indeed the Creator merely were to make something exist but a creature were to make it blessed. But since this is impossible, a creature cannot free another creature from sin. Even some little sin burdens every creature. Since the lightest sin is opposed to God, God is then greater than every creature. No creature, as a result, is adequate to compensate for even the least sin.

Leo: If sin, as you say, is so weighty we are in the greatest danger, because we sin daily.

Why God imposed a punishment upon man that did not suffice to remove sin

Leo: But why did God impose a punishment upon the sinner if the punishment is not adequate for the sin?

Odo: For the remission of sins.[14] Now, all punishments of this sort — for example, the patient enduring of all burdens, various chastisements of the body and soul, and all other things that arouse one to do the good — can, without providing full compensation for sin, only bring one to forgiveness, but not to glory.

That man was made in order to complete the heavenly city

Leo: How then can man offer satisfaction for sin, or how can he compensate for sin, if the whole creature is inadequate [compensation] and does not suffice to remove the sin?

Odo: He cannot in any way, by himself.

Leo: Our debate of Reason has come to this, then: if a man escapes punishments through forgiveness of sins, still he does not arrive at glory. He enjoys a middle state in which he remains for eternity. As a result, angels who have not sinned remain in glory, while a man who receives remission for sin obtains a rest of this middle sort. But one who is without remission for sins incurs perpetual punishment. We arrived at the conclusion too that your Christ is in no way necessary for this world. For that [middle] state of rest is obtained without Christ and under the law, where we read about the remission of sins. And you, who proposed to reveal the power of your Christ, have proved instead that man does not in any way obtain glory.

Odo: I undertake to prove to you not only that man can, but even that it is necessary that man achieve the glory of angels. When I shall have done this with Christ's help I pray that, after having abandoned error, you will become a Christian.

Leo: Abandon your hope, but attempt to do what you promise.

Odo: It will become clear that man's glory is possible if it can be proved that it is necessary; for that which is necessary is also possible.

Leo: That is so.

Odo: I do believe that you will not deny the truth of what one reads about God in several places in Scripture: "All things whatsoever he has willed, he has done (Ps. 113b: 3 Vulg. and Ps. 134: 6 Vulg.)."

Leo: It is certainly true.

Odo: Moreover, God willed to make a heavenly city whose citizens, the angels, he created. God, being good, created none but good angels. Justly, those who were never made [evil] were cast out of that city.[15] So, with the city partly empty, the work that God began remained incomplete. Truly, though, God's plan cannot be brought to naught. It is necessary, then, for the city, which God began, to be completed, lest it be said that God foolishly began something which later he was unable or unwilling to complete. But it is wicked to ascribe a change of intention to God, or some weakness. So, God will complete what he began. For this reason he made man and gave him the power to propagate in order that he might complete what was begun. It is necessary, then, that God's plan be fulfilled through man. For, "All things whatsoever he has willed, he has done (Ps. 113b: 3 Vulg. and Ps. 134: 6 Vulg.)."

That the number of citizens in the heavenly city that must be completed is greater than the number of angels at the first creation

Leo: Because your explanation refers to the first creation, I ask whether the number of angels that were made then, before angels became evil, sufficed for the completion of the city.

Odo: It seems not. For if the number of angels who were created would alone suffice, man might replace those who fell and would be in a position to rejoice over the fall of those who fell, whose glory he may obtain. Since no one but the just may enter heavenly glory, how can one be just who will rejoice at another's sin?[16] For this reason we say that for God [i.e., for the divine plan] the number that must complete the city is greater than the number of angels at the first creation. Truly man was made so that, even if all the angels had remained just, the remainder for the city would be[17] drawn from among men; if they [all] should fall, then the whole would be completed from mankind.

That God alone can satisfy for sin

Leo: If God's plan cannot be frustrated, it is necessary that man be raised to the glory of angels. God however is omnipotent. Therefore everything he has planned, he can do. It is necessary then that man be raised to glory, but the previous arguments prove that that is impossible. How is that necessary, then, which is impossible? This is a contradiction of reason. When I consider God's plan, it is necessary for man to cross over to glory; when I consider man's weakness and God's justice, it is entirely impossible for man to come to glory. What is more contrary to the impossible than the necessary?

Odo: Let our Christ come, let him come, and dissolve this contradiction.

Leo: How?

Odo: Listen, if you will reconsider the things brought to light above,[18] it is satisfaction for sin alone that is an obstacle to man's glory. If he could offer satisfaction for sin, he could certainly attain glory. But man cannot do this. What then? Is that which man cannot do impossible in every way? Cannot God do what man cannot? If not, God would not be omnipotent. Therefore, God can offer satisfaction for sin.

Leo: How does God offer satisfaction for sin, when it does not pertain to him? How does he who has not sinned satisfy for sin? The sinner ought to offer satisfaction, not God.

Odo: Since it is necessary for man to obtain glory, which he cannot do without satisfaction, God can offer satisfaction but ought not to. Man ought to, but cannot. As a result, it is necessary for the natures of God and man to come together: that God become man, and that the one Jesus Christ become both God and man. He is not part God and part man, but the whole of what he is, is God, and the whole of what he is, is man.[19] He is man not by a confusion of natures, as if the one would be absorbed into the other, but with the integral property of each nature remaining in one true person. Jesus Christ is not then two, but in every sense is one indivisible person. Because he is God omnipotent, he can offer satisfaction for sin; because he is man he ought to. He can, as God; he ought to, as man.

That it is appropriate for Christ to offer satisfaction for sin, although he has not sinned

Leo: Why should he offer satisfaction when, even though he is a man, he is not — just as you say — a sinful man?

Odo: On account of compassion and mercy. Because we could not correct our sin, he corrected it for us, like a brother for his brothers, and he is of the same nature as we. There is nothing alien in his nature in condescending and offering satisfaction for us, who share his nature. On account of this identity of nature, then, he bears our sins — freely bearing wounds and death for our sins, which he did not have to do because he himself did not deserve such things. He feeds us with his flesh and blood, in order to unite us to him in one body, so that we are one with him and he is one with us. For this reason, he made our miseries his own, ascribed to himself our sins, and applied our words from the Psalms and the writings of the Prophets to his own person: "God, my God, why have you forsaken me? far from my salvation and from the words of my sins (Ps. 21: 2 Vulg.)." Yet in his own person he had not been forsaken by God, nor did he have any[20] sins. But because he reckons us as in him, he attributes to himself that which we have.

That Christ was able to give more than every sin's [penalty]

Leo: How does he offer satisfaction for man? How does he offer recompense for man's sin, for which the whole world does not suffice?

Odo: He gave the price — his own life — and suffered an undeserved punishment: death.

Leo: How could the life and death of one man compensate for sin, when the whole world is not enough?

Odo: You cannot deny[21] that nothing can be compared to God, or that God stands incomparably above all things. A human sin, then, cannot be compared to God because God is far more good than sin is evil. Since God gave his life, then, he gave a price that exceeds all sin. This price, if it were only equal to the sin, would suffice to remove it. But the more it is worth,[22] the more it satisfies.

Besides, if the life of God is better than all things, and death worse than all things, then it is necessary that if the generation of something is better, its corruption is worse. But Christ's life is a good beyond all things; his death then is an evil beyond every evil. Christ's death, consequently, is beyond every sin.[23] When Christ suffered death, then, he bore a punishment beyond every sin and greater than every sin would deserve. Therefore he who has suffered a penalty greater than the entire sin of the world — that is, death — and given a greater price — namely, his own life — has removed the entire sin of the world. He is the lamb who takes away the sin of the world (Jn. 1: 29). This is the sacrifice which, once offered, removes the sins of all the just: from the start, sins from the past, the present, and the future even unto the end of the world.[24] This sacrifice he mercifully offered for us, so that the victim who offers himself always for us to the Father in heaven, we might sacrifice continually to the Father on earth: not by putting him to death again, but by remembering with the greatest devotion his death offered for the remission of sins, for the living just as for the dead.

After receiving the remission of sins it remains that we proceed through various acts of justification along the right path to heaven, once Christ has offered complete satisfaction for sin. As a result, that satisfaction would be effective only for those to whom remission has been granted, with the cooperation of their own merits or the merits of their neighbors. Christ's satisfaction profits nothing for the one who cannot receive remission for sin. For that reason, "they are blessed whose iniquities have been remitted (Ps. 31: 1 Vulg.)." For if someone's sin is forgiven, there is no reason why he should be excluded from the kingdom [of glory], once satisfaction has been fulfilled by Christ. Therefore, our Christ is most necessary for the world, for without him no man can come to that glory for which he was made. Remission for sin under the law is not adequate unless Christ's satisfaction follow in the Gospel. For this reason, although sins were forgiven for the ancient patriarchs and the prophets, still they were not in glory until satisfaction for sin was fulfilled through Christ's passion.

Leo: Where were they?

Odo: In a place suitable for the just of this age, yet not in glory.

Leo: I do not have a reasonable objection for one who argues reasonably. Nevertheless, I do not believe you lest, deceived by the subtlety or cunning of words, I might stray from the very firm ground of the holy law.

Whether grace exists where there is necessity

Leo: But why should God be credited with your salvation if he is led to this out of necessity? Surely he requires the salvation of humanity, upon which the strength of his plan depends. If he does not save man, he reveals the weakness and false nature of his plan. If only to avoid something so unbefitting, it is necessary then that he bring about man's salvation.

Odo: Indeed, it is necessary to pay what it was not necessary to promise. One who freely promises something obligates himself to pay with a certain necessity. Although there is some necessity afterward, nevertheless before the promise payment is an act of grace and of the will. This necessity that proceeds from grace, however, must not be separated from grace itself. As a result it is right to say that an act is performed by grace which in the first place had been promised with abundant grace.

Why God, who gave every good, did not owe satisfaction for sin

Leo: In this respect, what you said above disturbs me: that God ought not offer satisfaction for sin unless he becomes man. Now, satisfaction for sin is a great good. But every good comes from him who is the highest good. How then can you say that God ought not do what it is his nature to do? Who owes good more than he, from whom every good comes? So God, who owes every good, owes the good of satisfaction.

Odo: God ought, and ought not, because a debt is spoken of in two ways. There is the debt of grace and the debt of merit. Perhaps I ought to assist one person because he deserves it (*meritis suis*), and another according to my love. Similarly, perhaps I ought to suffer either because I have sinned, and then justifiably, or for the sake of love alone on behalf of another. In the same way, God did not owe satisfaction for sin because he deserves to (*merito*), since he did not himself deserve to for his own sin, nor did man deserve it because of his own righteousness. Still, God "owed" satisfaction for the sake of love alone. So, God did not have to offer satisfaction according to a debt of merit but had to offer satisfaction according to a debt of grace. When I said above that God alone could offer satisfaction, but did not have to, and that man could not but did have to,[25] in each case the "owing" must be understood as the "debt of merit." God did not have to *ex merito* while man did have to *ex merito*. In this sense it is true that God does not owe satisfaction for the sin of man unless he is man. Yet because God is made man—even though this ought to be attributed to ineffable grace—nevertheless merit is so fully distributed in the satisfaction of the debt that, because he was made man and the brother of men, justly he does not despise his nature in man but like a brother would give assistance to brothers and justly offer satisfaction for his brothers.

How God was made man from a virgin without harm from the impurity of a woman

Leo: In one thing especially we laugh at you and think that you are crazy. You say that God was conceived within his mother's womb, surrounded by a vile fluid, and suffered enclosure within this foul prison for nine months when finally, in the tenth month, he emerged from her private parts (who is not embarrassed by such a scene!). Thus you attribute to God what is most unbecoming, which we would not do without great embarrassment.

Odo: God fills all things and is everywhere whole. Although he fills us[27] and is whole even in us who are sinners, he is untouched by the uncleanness of our sins, but remains uncontaminated and pure. He sees all things and nothing hurts him. He sees darkness yet remains untouched by the darkness, since "light shines in darkness" (Jn. 1: 5)" and "night, just like day, will be illuminated (Ps. 138: 12 Vulg.)." The Most Pure sees sin, and the Most Just sees our injustices, since he justly orders every evil he sees. The light of justice is not extinguished by making sins visible, just as the light of this world shines upon the sordid fleshly body but is not soiled by it. Why then are you offended if God is conceived in a virgin, when he preserves his purity everywhere?

Moreover, there are two ways by which we judge all things: sense and reason. But reason judges in one way and sense in another. For sense judges by usefulness, pleasure, desire, and their contraries. We prefer the usual to the unusual, the useful to the harmful, and that which pleases us agreeably to that which disagreeably offends. Reason investigates the nature of things more subtly. Reason prefers animated things to inanimate, sensible to insensible, and heavenly to earthly.[28] Too hastily does a peasant prefer that a snake disappear from the cleft of a rock than that the rock disappear from his wall, being mindful of desire and what is agreeable to look upon, because the sight of a serpent is horrible but the sight of a rock is not horrible. But reason truly prefers a serpent to a rock, however precious. Sense prefers the best house to a fruitbearing tree, so that it prefers that a tree be cut down than that a house burn down. But truly reason prefers the live tree to the inanimate house. A peasant would rather have many beasts perish in the woods than lose one coin from his purse, although reason does not regard any coin as comparable in value to an animal. The peasant would prefer that many stars fall from heaven rather than one shrub perish in his field, although reason properly places heavenly things above earthly things.[29]

So too our sense despises our genitalia, viscera, and excrement, and judges them unclean. Reason, however, judges nothing unclean but sin, because God created all things good (Gen. 1: 10). The Gospel of the lord Jesus attests to this: "It does not defile a man to eat with dirty hands (Matt. 15: 20)." "All that enters the mouth goes to the stomach and so is discharged into the drain,[30] and does not defile a man. Those things which go forth from the heart — theft, murder, adultery — these things defile a man (cf. Matt. 15: 17–19)." Our apostle — first one of you, a Jew and instructed in the law, who then rose up against you who judge that certain foods are unclean according to the law — agrees with this: "Every creature of God is good, and nothing ought to be rejected that is received with thanksgiving (1 Tim. 4: 4)." More, although the law judges many things unclean according to sense, consider that the Gospel of the lord Jesus and the doctrine of his apostles says that every creature is good and clean in the judgement of reason. Reason is preferred to sense and judges the senses. Sense, however, cannot aspire to reason but often considers the subtle judgement of reason foolish and insane.

We, however, having put off the sense of the flesh, think of the human body according to the direction of reason: that it is joined to a person's mind in unity and will dwell with it in eternal unity, forever a participant in honor or glory. We consider the body as cleaner than the moon,[31] more precious than the sun, destined for the [last] judgement to which it will have to submit together with its mind, whether to glory or to punishment, thereby manifesting in itself God's eternal mercy or suffering his justice; now it is an animal-like body but at the [last] judgement it will be spiritual.

How far is such a prerogative raised up among bodies? If I compare the heaven, it is not appropriate. If I consider the splendor of the sun and stars, precious to the eye, it appears to be less so. What truly is sense? In so great a matter, the rude person is not afraid to disparage what displeases him. Sight is horrified by the appearance of the genitalia, the nose mocks the odor, touch flees from the filth. But consider that this is the judgement of sense regarding something to which even heaven cannot be compared.

If our body is such as this, we who are sinners, what shall we say of body of the virgin from whom the lord was born? Clearly the holy angel

Gabriel said that she is "full of grace (Lk. 1: 28)." If full, nothing of hers was in any way devoid of grace. So, nothing of hers was emptied by sin, whose whole being was filled with grace. Therefore her sex was filled with glory, her womb was filled with glory, her organs were filled with glory, the whole of her was filled with glory, because the whole of her was filled with grace.[32] Truly that woman surpassed sense; she was wise who said: "Blessed is the womb which bore you, and the breasts which gave you suck (Lk. 11: 27)."

Where is that which you called the uncleanness of woman, the obscene prison, the fetid womb? Confess, you wretch, your stupidity. Was she endowed with sense with the animals but without reason among men? In his conception this virgin became the marriage bed of omnipotent God and the sanctuary of the Holy Spirit. In her, God dwelled in a unique fashion and in a manner other than in the highest spirits of celestial virtue. The secret places of her blessed womb were the more holy, or rather the more divine, the more intimately divine mysteries grew there. It is the blessed virgin from whose womb were taken up the seeds which became God. What in all creation is more holy, more clean, more pure[33] than the virgin from whom was assumed what God became? O womb, O flesh, in whom and from whom the creator was created, and God was made incarnate. Certainly, we prefer all other human bodies to every [other kind of] body. However, I prefer the body of the most Blessed Virgin even to angelic spirits. From this [body] God willed to take what eventually he united inseparably to himself, by which he redeemed the earth and restored heaven, by which the infernal regions were despoiled, the earth healed, and the heavens perfected — for all of which he did not choose a heavenly spirit.

Leo: I hear what I have not heard before so fully articulated; before this, I did not know that you have the support of so many reasoned arguments.

Odo: Why then don't you believe us?

Leo: Because I do not dare to entrust the truth of our heritage to your words.

Odo: Brother Acard, I presented these reasoned arguments to the Jew regarding the advent of Christ, because some people urged me to argue more subtly for certain Catholics who had sided with the views of the Jew.

Notes

Introduction: Odo of Tournai

1. See *Renaissance and Renewal in the Twelfth Century*, ed. Robert L. Benson and Giles Constable (Cambridge, MA: Harvard University Press, 1982).

2. *Herimanni Liber de restauratione monasterii Sancti Martini Tornacensis*, in MGH, SS, 14 (Hanover, 1883; reprint, 1963), 266–317. (References to this work will supply page and line numbers to this edition.) Herman was elected abbot in 1127 following the death of his predecessor, Segardus. After approximately ten years, Herman stepped down as abbot, according to one account, or was forced to resign, according to another. Regardless of the circumstances that brought him to abdicate as abbot, he continued to work on behalf of Tournai. In 1142 he was in Rome seeking for the chapter the right of electing the bishop, and it was there that he began this history, soon after the fiftieth anniversary of the restoration of the monastery of St. Martin of Tournai. For a good discussion of the older sources treating Odo and the monastery of St. Martin of Tournai, see especially Ursmer Berlière, *Monasticon Belge* (Abbaye de Maredsous, 1897) 1/a: 271–273.

3. *Amandus de Castello de Odonis episcopi Cameracensis vita vel moribus*, in MGH, SS, 15, 2 (Hanover, 1883; reprint, 1963): 942–945.

4. *Liber de restauratione*, 307, 6. For more information on this foundation for women, see pp. 15–16 above.

5. "Monumenta Historiae Tornacensis," in MGH, SS, 14: 266.

6. Herman was related by blood to a long list of bishops or abbots, and to the counts of Flanders. Equally important, Herman traveled widely on behalf of the monastery (of which he later became abbot) and the bishopric of Tournai, and acquired extensive knowledge of events in the larger world. Since he had been well educated — acquainted with Virgil, Sallust, and the Roman historians as well as the Bible and the fathers of the Church — Herman was able to refer to older histories and chronicles in order to expand his treatment of the monastery at Tournai. His personal experience and his access to historical source materials render Herman's work valuable both as a vita or biography of Odo of Tournai and as a chronicle of events in Flanders and, indeed, Europe as a whole. In the words of Charles Dereine, "A work of a well informed and, from our point of view, impartial man, the *Liber* constitutes a document of the greatest value." See his "Odon de Tournai et la crise du cénobitisme au XIe siècle," *Revue du Moyen Âge Latin* 4 (1948): 140.

7. *Liber de restauratione*, 274, 43.

8. "Erat quippe fundatus grammatica, rhetorica ornatus, armatus dialectica." Amand du Chastel, *De Odonis episcopi*, 943, 43. This text is reproduced by

Léopold Delisle in *Rouleaux des morts du XIᵉ au XVᵉ siècle* (Paris: Libraire de la Société de l'Histoire de France, 1866), 171–177.

9. For a history of this chapter at Notre Dame, see Jacques Pycke, *Le Chapitre cathédral Notre-Dame de Tournai de la fin du XIᵉ à la fin du XIIIᵉ siècle*, Recueil de Travaux d'Histoire et de Philologie 6, 30 (Brussels: Université de Louvain, 1986). For Odo's relations with the chapter, see especially 111–113.

10. *Liber de restauratione*, 274, 48–49.

11. For this early history of Tournai, see "Tournai" in the *Dictionnaire des Églises de France* (5 vols.; Paris: Robert Laffont, 1966–1971) 5: 120–127.

12. It was for the purpose of persuading the papacy to grant this independence to Tournai that Herman traveled to Rome in 1142. See *Liber de restauratione*, 274, 23.

13. *Liber de restauratione*, 277, 39–48.

14. F.J. Labis, "Le bienheureaux Odon, évêque de Cambrai," *Revue Catholique de Louvain* 14 (1856): 445.

15. Herman explains that Odo could often be seen in the evenings before the church with his students, pointing out to them the stars, the movements of the Zodiac, and the milky way. The cultural rebirth at Tournai, then, was not confined to the *trivium*, but included the *quadrivium* as well, that is the entire course of a liberal arts curriculum. *Liber de restauratione*, 275, 1–3.

16. *Liber de restauratione*, 276, 19.

17. For this gloss to the *Categoriae decem* of Pseudo-Augustine found in a tenth-century Latin manuscript (Cod. lat. 843) in the imperial library in Vienna, see Carl Sigmund Barach, "Zur Geschichte des Nominalismus vor Roscellin," in *Kleine philosophische Schriften* (Vienna: Wilhelm Braumüller, 1878), 5–25. The text of the *Categoriae decem* can be found in *Arisoteles Latinus* 1.1–5, ed. L. Minio-Paulello (Bruges: Desclée de Brouwer, 1961): 133–175. For a good discussion of the influence of this Ps. Augustinian work on the early medieval understanding of universals, see especially John Marenbon, *From the Circle of Alcuin to the School of Auxerre: Logic, Theology, and Philosophy in the Early Middle Ages* (Cambridge: Cambridge University Press, 1981), chapter 1. Although there seems to be some agreement that a quasi-nominalism appears in the Carolingian age, there is far less agreement once one attempts to identify with precision its nature and its proponents. For a somewhat polemical treatment of the history of nominalism before Roscelin, see Joseph Reiners, *Der Nominalismus in der Frühscholastik: Ein Beitrag zur Geschichte der Universalienfrage im Mittelalter* (Münster: Aschendorff, 1910).

18. Even for this later movement, however, opinion regarding the nature of nominalism is shifting. See especially William J. Courtenay, "Nominalism and Late Medieval Thought: A Bibliographical Essay," *Theological Studies* 33(1972): 716–734, reprinted in Courtenay's *Covenant and Causality in Medieval Thought* (London: Variorum Reprints, 1984); and see Heiko A. Obermann, "*Via Antiqua* and *Via Moderna*: Late Medieval Prolegomena to Early Reformation Thought," *Journal of the History of Ideas* 48(1987): 23–40.

19. See Marenbon, *From the Circle of Alcuin to the School of Auxerre*, 7.

20. Abelard's views on universals brought him into open conflict with William of Champeaux in Paris at the beginning of the twelfth century. His position is

well set out in his glosses entitled *Logica "Ingredientibus"* (commentaries on Porphyry's *Isagoge* and Aristotle's *On Interpretation* and *Categories*). A selection from Abelard's work is translated under the title "On Universals" in *Medieval Philosophy from St. Augustine to Nicholas of Cusa*, ed. John F. Wippel and Alan B. Wolter (New York: Free Press, 1969), 190–203. For a useful summary of the different opinions regarding the nature of universals during the first half of the twelfth century, see especially John of Salisbury's *Metalogicon* 2.17. This section is reprinted in translation in *Philosophy in the Middle Ages*, ed. Arthur Hyman and James J. Walsh (Indianapolis: Hackett Publishing Co., 1977), 167–69. John's defense of logic in the *Metalogicon* is aimed at both those who disparaged it (so-called Cornificians) and its naive advocates. See E.K. Tolan, "John of Salisbury and the Problem of Medieval Humanism," *Études d'Histoire Littéraire et Doctrinale*, 4th ser. 19 (Montréal: Institut d'Études Médiévales, 1968), 189–199.

21. "Aristoteli an Platoni magis credendum putatis? Magna est utriusque auctoritas, quatenus vix audeat quis alterum alteri dignitate preferre." See *Epistola ad Augienses* 11.10–15, ed. Karl Manitius, MGH, Quellen zur Geistesgeschichte des Mittelalters, 2/1 (Weimar: Hermann Böhlaus Nachfolger, 1958), 40. Like most early medieval thinkers, Gunzo decides in favor of Plato. See *Epistola* 5.11–15 (p. 29) and Manitius's introduction, 10, n. 2.

22. For Boethius's text, see his *In Isagogen Porphyrii Commenta*, ed. George Schepss, CSEL 48 (Leipzig, 1906; reprint, Johnson Reprint Co., 1966). For an English translation of Porphyry's text, which represents his commentary on Aristotle's *Categories*, see *Porphyry the Phoenician: Isagoge*, trans., intro and notes by Edward W. Warren (Toronto: Pontifical Institute of Mediaeval Studies, 1975). For the Middle Ages, this text was basic to a philosophical education. Isidore of Seville describes it as "an introduction for those beginning philosophy" ("*Isagoge* quippe Graece, Latine introductio dicitur, eorum scilicet qui philosophiam incipiunt.") See his *Etymologies Book II* 2.25.1, ed. Peter K. Marshall (Paris: Société d'Édition "Les Belles Lettres," 1983), 110.

23. On the meaning of *antiqui* and the emerging conflict with the *moderni*, see especially L.M. De Rijk, *Logica Modernorum* (Assen: Van Gorcum, 1962), 1: 14–17.

24. Presumably Porphyry's *Isagoge*, which Boethius had translated in two versions. Again, see, Boethius's *In Isagogen Porphyrii Commenta*, CSEL 48. Boethius was himself enjoying a sort of revival. See the old but still useful work of A. Van de Vyver. "Les étapes du développement philosophique du haut moyen-âge," *Revue Belge de Philologie et d'Histoire* 8 (1929): 425–452.

25. For a discussion of such attacks, see my "Attitudes Towards Philosophy and Dialectic During the Gregorian Reform," *Journal of Religious History* 16/2 (1990): 115–125.

26. Although Abelard does not criticize Roscelin, his former teacher, by name, he likely has him in view when he attacks certain dialecticians who appeal to the authority of the Peripatetics but only succeed in undermining Trinitarian dogma. See his *Tractatus de unitate et trinitate*, in François Picavet, *Roscelin, philosophe et théologien* (Paris: Félix Alcan, 1911), 125–127. Roscelin's views were also attacked for undermining the Trinitarian dogma in the second decade of the twelfth century

by the Benedictine monk Rupert of Deutz, in his *De divinis officiis*. For a discussion, see John Van Engen, *Rupert of Deutz* (Berkeley: University of California Press, 1983), 75–78.

27. See Picavet, *Roscelin, philosophe et théologien*, 118–119.

28. *Liber de restauratione*, 275, 38.

29. Anselm's remark can be found in his *Epistola de incarnatione Verbi* 1 (*Opera omnia* 2: 9). It is reprinted in Picavet's *Roscelin, philosophe et théologien*, 120. The way one understands this remark, however, and how it illustrates Anselm's own views on the nature of universals, is much at issue. Jasper Hopkins points out that this same passage has led to "four different interpretations of Anselm's theory of universals," which range from something like what is called nominalism to extreme realism. See *Anselm of Canterbury*, ed. and trans. Jasper Hopkins (4 vols.; New York: Edwin Mellen Press, 1974–76), 4: 58, and all of chapter 3: "The Anselmian Theory of Universals."

30. On prohibitions against laughter in schools and monastic precincts, see my "*Risus monasticus*: Laughter and Medieval Monastic Culture," *Revue Bénédictine* 97, 1/2 (1987): 90–100.

31. *Liber de restauratione*, 274, 52–53.

32. "in quo solvit, si unum idemque sit res et ens." *Liber de restauratione*, 275, 8–10. Without knowing the content of this treatise, it is very difficult to know precisely how to translate *res* and *ens*. Given the background of the controversy over universals, substance is a reasonable choice for *res*, even though Odo does employ the Latin *substantia* as well.

33. Others doubted whether Odo's discipline was religious, Herman notes, inasmuch as "some would say that he [Odo] applied this stricture not on behalf of religion, but according to the ancient custom of [the schools of] philosophy" ("Quamvis autem nonnulli dicerent, eum hanc districtionem non exercere causa religionis, sed potius antique philosophie consuetudinis."). *Liber de restauratione*, 276, 10–12.

34. For a fuller discussion of Odo's conversion and the eremitic movement of the late eleventh century, see my "Odo of Tournai and Peter Damian: Poverty and Crisis in the Eleventh Century," *Revue Bénédictine* 98, 1/2 (1988): 114–140.

35. "[*De libero arbitrio*] quem magister ob solum bibliotece sue comparans subplementum, in scrinio cum ceteris libris proiecit, utpote qui adhuc mundane sapientie deditus magis delectabatur lectione Platonis quam Augustini." *Liber de restauratione*, 276, 16–18.

36. See Augustine, *De libero arbitrio*, 3.3.6.21–22. The Latin text to *De libero arbitrio* will be found in Augustine's *Opera*, ed. W.M. Green, CCSL 29 (Turnhout: Brepols, 1970), 212–321. For a translation of the entire work, see *On the Free Choice of the Will*, trans. with intro. and notes by Thomas Williams (Indianapolis: Hackett Publishing Co., 1993). My references are to the edition in CCSL.

37. Herman notes that prior to his conversion Odo called himself, and was known to others, as Odardus. *Liber de restauratione*, 275, 12.

38. "cum ecce legendo ad tercium librum pervenitur, in quo prefatus doctor servo pro criminibus suis de priori dignitate pulso et mundande cloace deputato comparat peccatrices animas, que celestem quidem gloriam pro sceleribus suis

perdunt, hunc vero mundum cloace fetide similem quodammodo decorant, quamdiu in eo vivunt. Hanc ergo sententiam cum magister Odardus audientibus discipulis legisset, tactus nimio dolore cordis intrinsecus et ex imo pectoris trahens alta suspiria: "Heu," inquit, "quam fortiter ista nos premit sententia! Hec re vera tam proprie mihi videtur nobis congruere, asci propter nos solummodo fuerit scripta. Hunc siquidem fetidum mundum quantulacumque scientia nostra perornamus, celesti vero gloria post mortem digni non erimus, quoniam nullum Deo servicium facimus nec scientiam nostram in eius famulatu expendimus, sed in seculi vanitate pro mundana laude male ipsa abutimur." Hiis dictis, surrexit, totusque lacrimis perfusus, ecclesiam intravit. Tota subito scola turbatur, canonicorum etiam conventus admiratione nimia concutitur." *Liber de restauratione*, 276, 26–37. For Augustine's comparison of the soul to a slave, see *De libero arbitrio*, 3.1.2.8.

39. "Clericis vero magistri canonicorum magis quam monachorum ordinem placet assumere, quia et in ecclesiasticis officiis et in cotidiano victu seu vestitu canonici tolerabiliorem ritum ducerent quam monachi." *Liber de restauratione*, 277, 2–4. On the efforts to reform canonical life in this period, and the proliferation of religious options available to Odo and his followers, see pp. 10–14 above.

40. On eremitism in France, see Jean Becquet, "L'érémitisme clérical et laïc dans l'Ouest de la France," in *L'eremitismo in Occidente nei secoli XI e XII. Atti della settimana internazionale di studio* (Milan: Miscellanea del Centro di Studi Medioevali, 4, 1965), 182–211. For Romuald's influence, see especially Giovanni Tabacco, "Romualdo di Ravenna e gli inizi dell'eremitismo camaldolese," in *L'eremitismo in Occidente nei secoli XI e XII*, 73–121. Romuald greatly influenced Peter Damian, prior of Fonte Avellana and later Cardinal Bishop of Ostia. See Colin Phipps, "Romuald, Model Hermit. Eremitical Theory in Saint Peter Damian's 'Vita Beati Romualdi,' chapters 16–27" in *Monks, Hermits, and the Ascetic Tradition*, ed. W.J. Sheils, Studies in Church History 22 (Oxford: B. Blackwell, 1985), 65–77. For the significance of the community at Pomposa as a link between Romuald and Damian, see Dante Balboni, "San Pier Damiano, Maestro e Discepolo in Pomposa," *Benedictina* 22(1975): 73–89.

41. The sense that the monasteries no longer offered the most secure route to realize the evangelical precepts, thereby prompting the appearance of new alternatives, is nicely summarized in M.D. Chenu, *Nature, Man, and Society in the Twelfth Century*, trans. Jerome Taylor and Lester K. Little (Chicago: University of Chicago Press, 1968), 202–238.

42. For a fuller examination of criticism of Benedictine liturgical practices among eremitic reformers, see my "Peter Damian on Cluny, Liturgy, and Penance," *Journal of Religious History* 15/1 (1988): 61–75; reprinted in *Studia Liturgica* 18/2 (1988): 170–187.

43. One of the more accessible studies of the eremitic movement in this period remains Henrietta Leyser's *Hermits and the New Monasticism: A Study of Religious Communities in Western Europe 1000–1150* (New York: St. Martin's Press, 1984).

44. A process Milis calls the "cenobitisation" of eremitic houses. See Ludo Milis, "Ermites et chanoines réguliers au XIIᵉ siècle," *Cahiers de Civilisation Médiévale* 22 (1979): 61. There is of course a certain paradox involved in speaking of eremitic *communities*. If one insists on defining a hermit as a recluse and isolated

individual, then the term is only poorly understood. In fact the religious hermits in Europe in the eleventh and twelfth centuries also placed importance upon community life. The term is equally problematic if, based on its etymology, one understands it to imply a flight to the desert, which certainly did not exist in any real sense in France, England, or elsewhere in Europe. For a discussion of terminology, see Jean Leclercq, "'Eremus' et 'eremita.' Pour l'histoire du vocabulaire de la vie solitaire," *Collectanea Ordinis Cisterciensis Reformatorum* 25 (1963): 8–30.

45. See J.L. Dickinson, "Canons Regular of St. Augustine," *New Catholic Encyclopedia* 3: 62–64.

46. As Caroline Walker Bynum has shown, twelfth-century treatises recommending the life of canons regular tend to emphasize this sense of mutual responsibility: that each is enjoined to assist in the edification of others not only through preaching but also by personal example. See her *Docere Verbo et Exemplo: An Aspect of Twelfth Century Spirituality* (Missoula, MT: Scholars Press, 1979), especially chapter 1.

47. See, for example, the work of Romuald's biographer and disciple, Peter Damian, whose *Opusculum* 14, *Contra clericos regulares proprietarios* (PL 145), attacks those canons who would defend their possession of private property and recalls them to the model of the primitive community of apostles in Jerusalem, among whom all goods were to be held in common. For Damian's biography of Romuald, one may consult the *Vita Romualdi*, ed. Giovanni Tabacco, Fonti per la Storia d'Italia no. 94 (Rome: Istituto Storico Italiano per il Medio Evo, 1957).

48. For a more complete discussion of the reform of the life of canons regular in the eleventh and early twelfth century, see especially Jean Châtillon, "La crise de l'Église aux XIᵉ et XIIᵉ siècles et les origines des grandes fédérations canoniales," *Revue d'Histoire de la Spiritualité* 53 (1977): 3–46. In addition, one may consult Charles Dereine's classic study, "Chanoines," *Dictionnaire d'Histoire et de Géographie Ecclésiastiques*, ed. Alfred Baudrillart, et al. (Paris: Letouzey et Ane, 1912–) 12: 350–405. Also useful is Aloysius Smith, "Chanoines réguliers," *Dictionnaire de Spiritualité* 2: 463–477. On the spiritual life of canons regular see Jean Leclercq's "La spiritualitie des chanoines reguliers" in *La vita commune del clero nei secoli XI e XII* (Milan: Miscellanea del Centro di Studi Medioevali 3, 1959), 1: 117–135.

49. The literature treating this "crisis" for Benedictine monasticism is vast. The more important works are Charles Dereine, "Odon de Tournai et la crise du cénobitisme au XIᵉ siècle" *Revue du Moyen Âge Latin* 4 (1948): 137–154; Jean Leclercq, "The Monastic Crisis of the Eleventh and Twelfth Centuries," in *Cluniac Monasticism in the Central Middle Ages*, ed. Noreen Hunt (Hamden, CT: Archon Books, 1971), 217–237; and Norman Cantor, "The Crisis of Western Monasticism, 1050–1130," *American Historical Review* 66 (1960): 47–61. For a challenge to the notion of a crisis of monasticism, see John Van Engen, "The 'Crisis of Cenobitism' Reconsidered. Benedictine Monasticism in the Years 1050–1150," *Speculum* 61 (1986): 269–304.

50. On the early history of the community at St. Martin of Tournai, see the article "Ancienne abbatiale Saint-Martin," *Dictionnaire des Églises de France* (5 vols.; Paris: Robert Laffont, 1966–71), 5: 127–128. For Herman's account of the foundation of St. Martin's see especially the *Liber de restauratione*, 294–297.

51. "respondebat ille, se nullum invenire, qui in tanta paupertate vellet introire," *Liber de restauratione*, 278, 33.

52. Ibid., 279.

53. Ibid., 289, 47–48.

54. See my "Odo of Tournai and Peter Damian," 128–140.

55. "Vere, bone magister, idem vobis non solum de isto iuvene, sed etiam de aliis fratribus vestris sepius continget, nisi monachi efficiamini. Juxta urbem enim habitatis, et facile fratres vestri iuniores a secularibus clericis sociis suis decepti ad seculum reducentur, quia unus idemque vester et ipsorum est habitus; si autem monachi essetis, postea nullum de vestris temptarent reducere, quoniam, cum monachorum niger sit habitus, clericorum vero candidus, tanto horrori clerici habent habitum monachorum, ut quem semel viderint monachum numquam deinceps dignentur habere socium. Considera etiam, quod mollior et remissior sit vita clericorum, etiam regulariter viventium, quippe cum lineis induantur, carnibus frequenter vescantur, festis diebus nonnisi novem lectiones legant. . . . magis consulerem tibi clericisque tuis rigidiorem quam remissiorem expetere ordinem." *Liber de restauratione*, 290, 12–23. On the role of the community at Anchin in the monastic life of this area, see especially Charles Dereine, "Ermites, reclus et recluses dans l'ancien diocèse de Cambrai entre Scarpe et Haine (1075–1125)," *Revue Bénédictine* 97 (1987): 289–313.

56. *Liber de restauratione*, 278, 40.

57. Ibid., 299, 37–38.

58. "Post hunc vero Henricum videres mirum in modum iuvenes et virgines, senes cum iunioribus de tota provincia seculo relicto ad conversionem venientes." Ibid., 305, 37–38.

59. Jean Becquet notes that most eremitic communities at this time received women, either in separate houses or in double monasteries. See his "L'érémitisme clérical et laïc dans l'Ouest de la France," 195. For a good discussion of the role of laywomen in religious life, see Nicolas Huyghebaert, "Les femmes laïques dans la vie religieuse des XIᵉ et XIIᵉ siècles dans la province ecclésiastique de Reims," in *I laici nella "Societas Christiana" dei secoli XI e XII* (Milan: Miscellanea del Centro di Studi Medioevali 5, 1965), 346–395. While women were received into many eremitic communities, still these represented only a small portion of the total number of religious communities, most of which were open only to men. On some of the difficulties women faced in eremitic communities, see Henrietta Leyser, *Hermits and the New Monasticism*, 49–53. For Herman's identification of these new converts at St. Martin's, see *Liber de restauratione*, 306, 49–307, 42.

60. *Liber de restauratione*, 307, 1.

61. "non cruces aureas fabricare cupiebat, sed omnem qui sibi deferebatur pecuniam egentibus et oppressis erogabat." Ibid., 306, 17–18.

62. For this text, see the anonymous *De viris illustribus monasterii Sancti Martini Tornacensis*, ed. Ursmer Berlière, in *Studien und Mittheilungen aus dem Benedictiner und dem Cistercienser Orden* 12(1891), 93. While Odo's rejection of ecclesiastical revenues suggests his dedication to the ideal of apostolic poverty, it may also reflect a fear of even the suspicion of simoniac practices. Simony, which can be broadly defined as providing ecclesiastical preferment in exchange for a gift of

any sort, was a charge even brought against the Bishop, Rabod II. Although Rabod defended his innocence by taking an oath on the gospels, his unpleasant death soon after seemed to suggest a sort of divine judgment. Cf. *Liber de restauratione*, 309, 9.

63. "Et si quidem tunc altaris que ipsi tenuerant recipere voluisset, forsitan usque hodie ecclesia nostra exinde ditior esse potuisset; sed quia proposuerat nec altaria nec ecclesias vel decimas accipere, sed solummodo de labore manuum suarum et de agricultura quadrigarum nutrimentisque pecorum suorum vivere, nichil ex ecclesiasticis redditibus quos ipsi tenuerant voluit habere, dicens, talia non a monachis, sed solummodo a clericis possideri debere." *Liber de restauratione*, 306, 40–45.

64. Charles Dereine, "Odon de Tournai et la crise du cénobitisme au XIe siècle," 154. On the importance of manual labor to the eremitic reform movement, see Étienne Delaruelle, "Les ermites et spiritualité populaire," in *L'eremitismo in Occidente nei secoli XI e XII. Atti della settimana internazionale di studio* (Milan: Miscellanea del Centro di Studi Medioevali 4, 1965), 230.

65. See *Liber de restauratione*, 307, 33.

66. See my "Odo of Tournai and Peter Damian," 137–140.

67. *Liber de restauratione*, 308, 1.

68. Albert D'Haenens, "Moines et clercs à Tournai au début du XIIe siècle," in *La vita comune del clero nei secoli XI e XII, atti della Settimana di studio: Mendola, settembre 1959* (2 vols.; Milan: Miscellanea del Centro di Studi Medioevali 3, 1959), 2: 93–96.

69. Odo's community created an extensive library. For the contents of this library, see André Boutemy, "Odon d'Orléans et les origines de la bibliothèque de l'abbaye de Saint-Martin de Tournai," in *Mélanges dédiés à la mémoire de Félix Grat* (2 vols.; Paris: Mme. Pecquer-Grat, 1946–49), 2: 179–223. Herman provides a partial inventory of its contents in *Liber de restauratione*, 313, 4–9 as well as a list of codices copied by one of Odo's early companions, Godefrey (311, 41–46).

70. "eos obedientie vinculo constrictos," *Liber de restauratione*, 291, 39.

71. Ibid., 292, 11.

72. Ibid., 298, 18–20.

73. See Charles Dereine, "Ermites, reclus et recluses," 299–300.

74. *Liber de restauratione*, 293, 9.

75. Ibid., 295, 1–5.

76. Ibid., 316, 1.

77. Ibid., 317, 13.

78. Ibid., 317, 44–45.

79. Albert D'Haenens remarks that "Saint-Martin comptait, à la fin du XIIIe siècle, parmi les abbayes bénédictines les plus peuplées d'Europe occidentale. . . . A la fin du XIIIe siècle, Saint-Martin de Tournai connaisait donc une époque de splendeur." *L'Abbaye Saint-Martin de Tournai de 1290 à 1350* (Louvain: Publications Universitaires de Louvain, 1961), 91.

80. "ecce subito cecidit corona capitis nostri, et deficit gaudium cordis nostri." *Liber de restauratione*, 313, 32.

81. For a discussion, see Ernest Berteaux, *Étude historique de Cambrai, 500–1798* (2 vols.; Cambrai: impr. d'Halluin-Carlon, 1908). For a brief note on Odo, see 1:119–120.

82. Arras regained its independence with the support of Urban II, Phillip I of France, and Robert II, Count of Flanders, taking advantage of confusion in Cambrai when the episcopacy was claimed by two candidates — Manasses, brother of John I, Count of Soissons, who had been canonically elected, and Walcher, Henry IV's candidate. In 1094 Lambert, a canon of Lille, was elevated to the episcopacy in Arras, and its independence was ratified at the Council of Claremont in 1095. For a discussion, see M. Chartier, "Cambrai," *Dictionnaire d'Histoire et de Géographie Ecclésiastiques*, ed. Alfred Baudrillart et al. (Paris: Letouzey et Ane, 1912–) 11: 550–551.

83. On the commune of Cambrai, see Bryce Lyon, "Commune," *Dictionary of the Middle Ages* 3: 493–503. For the details of events relating to the commune in Cambrai, see the *Gesta episcoporum Cameracensium, versio Gallica* MGH SS, 7, 518–520.

84. See especially Alfred Cauchie, *La querelle des investitures dans les diocèses de Liège et de Cambrai*, par. 2 (Louvain: Charles Peeters, 1891), 196–206.

85. For Paschal's role, see Uta-Renate Blumenthal, *The Early Councils of Pope Paschal II, 1100–1110* (Toronto: Pontifical Institute of Mediaeval Studies, 1978), 73–79.

86. Herman insists that Henry V, attempting to gain the support of the papacy, ordered the people of Cambrai to expel Walcher and receive Odo (*Liber de restauratione*, 315, 5). Auger provides a different interpretation, and suggests that Walcher continued to enjoy Henry's support. See his "Odon de Cambrai," in *Biographie Nationale (de Belgique)* (Brussels: H. Thiry van Buggenhoudt, 1866–1986), 16:75–78.

87. See Blumenthal, *Pope Paschal II*, 79.

88. See Ursmer Berlière, *Monasticon Belge* (Liège: Centre National de Recherches d'Histoire Religieuse, 1964) 4/1–3: 692–93; 725.

89. "Erat enim mihi tunc Acquicinotus dulce refugium exsilii mei, quia potestate regia pellebar a sede Cameracensi, quod virgam et annulum, quae consecratus ab Ecclesia acceperam, dono imperatoris iterum accipere non acquiescebam." Odo of Tournai, *De blasphemia in Spiritum Sanctum*, PL 160: 1111D.

90. Auger remarks that Odo was forced to flee Cambrai as Henry V's armies approached. Cauchie adds that Walcher accompanied Henry and received the see of Cambrai from the emperor again, although he left with Henry when Henry departed from Cambrai. Odo then wished to return to Cambrai, but the townspeople feared the consequences and would not allow him to do so. As a result, Odo exercised his authority as bishop of Cambrai from the monastery of Anchin (see Cauchie, *La querelle*, 204–205). The sequence of events in this period, however, remains confused by the different accounts in our sources. For example, the *Gesta Odonis* gives an entirely different explanation for Odo's departure from Cambrai. Its anonymous author asserts that Odo, unwisely, accepted ring and staff from the emperor and was forced to leave Cambrai under suspicion by the pope. This account follows the *Gesta Galcheri*, and therefore one suspects that it may be partisan. See *Gesta Pontificum Cameracensium, Gestes des évêques de Cambrai de 1092 à 1138*, ed. Charles de Smedt (Paris: Société de l'Histoire de France, 1880), 112. Nevertheless, the *Gestorum versio Gallica* confirms this account, namely that Odo was forced to leave Cambrai at last not by Henry V but by Pope Paschal II, who

objected to the fact that Odo had received investiture from Henry. This version, in old French, treats Odo quite favorably as one who had increased the wealth and possessions of the see. It remains somewhat perplexing, then, that Odo should at one time be the reform candidate and at another time be expelled from his see by the papacy for having received investiture from the emperor. For the *Gestorum versio Gallica*, see *Gesta episcoporum Cameracensium* MGH, SS, 7 (Hanover, 1846; reprint, 1968), 510–525.

91. On Odo's death as an example of a "good death," see Henri Platelle, "La mort précieuse: La mort des moines d'après quelques sources des Pays Bas du sud," *Revue Mabillon* 60(1982): 156–158. The evidence that Odo died "well" would seem at the same time to undermine any suggestion that Odo may have been guilty of simony, and establishes a clear contrast to the fate of Rabod II, who, despite a formal acquittal on charges of simony, died a most unpleasant death. Cf. *Liber de restauratione*, 309, 30–31.

92. Or perhaps 29 June. For the date, see Rémy Ceillier, "Odon, Évêque de Cambrai," *Histoire générale des auteurs sacrés et ecclésiastiques* (Paris: L. Vives, 1858–63), 14: 73–74.

93. See *Bibliotheca Hagiographica Latina antiquae et mediae aetatis*, ed. Socii Bollandiani (2 vols.; Brussels: Socii Bollandiani, 1898–1901), 1: n. 6287f., p. 909.

94. *Liber de restauratione*, 275, 7–11.

95. *Amandus de Castello de Odonis episcopi Cameracensis vita vel moribus*, in *Rouleaux des morts du XIᵉ au XVᵉ siècle*, ed. Léopold Delisle, 176. Cf. Amand du Chastel, *De Odonis*, 945, 7–10.

96. For excerpts from this work by Godfrey, see PL 160: 1159–1160.

97. See John R. Williams, "Godfrey of Rheims, a Humanist of the Eleventh Century," *Speculum* 22(1947): 34.

98. See the literary note (from *Histoire Littéraire de la France* 9, 594) in PL 160: 1043C. André Wilmart refers to a poem in a Vatican codex entitled *De troiae excidio*, or *Planctus troiane destructionis*, in a thirteenth-century hand. However, he suggests it is the work of Odo of Orléans, not Odo of Cambrai. See *Bibliothecae Apostolicae Vaticanae: Codices Reginenses Latini*, vol. 2: codices 251–500, ed. André Wilmart (Vatican: Bibliotheca Vaticana, 1945), 344.

99. See "Odon, Évêque de Cambray," *Bibliothèque Générale des Écrivains de l'Ordre de S. Benoît*, ed. J. François (Bouillion: 1777–1778. 4 vols.; reprint Louvain-Héverlé: 1961), 2: 348.

100. For discussion and documentation, see an unpublished thesis by Paul Naedenoen, "Odon de Cambrai: Traité sur le canon de la Messe," (Université Catholique de Louvain: Institut Supérieur des Sciences Religieuses, 1969), xlv.

101. "Monumenta Historiae Tornacensis," in MGH, SS, 14, 268, 35–37; 269, 9–19.

102. For a brief note, see M.M. Lebreton, "Recherches sur les manuscrits des sermons de différents personnages du XIIᵉ siècle nommés Odon," *Bulletin d'information de l'Institut de recherche et d'histoire des textes* 3(1955): 34. Lebreton accepts the authenticity of both versions, although Martène, in his introduction to PL 160, considers that the first version may not be Odo's. Cf. PL 160: 1127.

103. PL 160: 1053–1070. For a discussion of Odo's *Expositio*, see Mary M.

Schaefer, "Twelfth Century Latin Commentaries on the Mass: The Relationship of the Priest to Christ and to the People," *Studia Liturgica* 15(1982–83): 76–86; and C.J. Destombes, "La tradition des Églises de Cambrai et d'Arras," *Revue des Sciences Ecclésiastiques* 4 (1861): 116–121.

104. PL 160: 1111–1118.

105. PL 160: 1118–1122.

106. So called by Émile Amann in his article in the *Dictionnaire de Théologie Catholique*, 11: 932.

107. PL 160: 1071–1102.

108. PL 160: 1103–1112.

109. PL 160: 1151–1160.

110. PL 171: 1213–1218. For a discussion of the attribution of this work, see Jean Leclercq, "Odo von Cambrai," *Lexikon für Theologie und Kirche*, ed. Josef Hofer and Karl Rahner (Freiburg: Herder, 1957–65), 7: 1099.

111. Boutemy remarks, "La sainteté d'Odon n'eût pas suffi à assurer ces succès et la mérite ne lui en appartient qu'en partie. Mais il est un domaine où son action exclusive fut prepondéronte: c'est la création d'une bibliothèque dont la développement en moins d'un siècle est digne d'admiration." See his "Odon d'Orléans et les origines de la bibliothèque de l'abbaye de Saint-Martin de Tournai," 186.

112. *Liber de restauratione*, 313, 8–9.

113. See Augustine, *Contra secundam Juliani responsionem opus imperfectum* 1.78 (PL 45: 1002) and 4.93 (PL 45: 1303), quoted by Jaroslav Pelikan, *The Christian Tradition: A History of Development and Doctrine*, vol. 1: *The Emergence of the Catholic Tradition (100–600)* (Chicago: University of Chicago Press, 1971), 313.

114. Augustine, *Epistle* 177.11, PL 33: 769. On the influence of Rom. 5:12 on the development of the doctrine of original sin, see S. Lyonnet, "Le Péché originel et l'exégèse de Rom. 5, 12–14," *Recherches de Science Religieuse* 44 (1956): 63–84.

115. Augustine, *Enchiridion ad Laurentium* (Leipzig: Tauchnitii, 1838), 27.

116. Augustine, *De diversis quaest. ad Simpl.*, ed. Almut Mutzenbecher, CCSL 44 (Turnhout: Brepols, 1970),1.2.16.

117. Augustine, *De diversis quaest. ad Simpl.* 83.68.3.

118. See especially R.J. O'Connell, "The Origin of the Soul in St. Augustine's Letter 143," *Revue des Études Augustiniennes* 28 (1982): 239–52. O'Connell continues his work in *The Origin of the Soul in St. Augustine's Later Works* (New York: Fordham University Press, 1987). Roland Teske has reviewed this work in *The Modern Schoolman* 66/1(1988): 71–78. For a good survey of views in the patristic era on the origin of the soul—and their later influence—see J.M. da Cruz Pontes, "Le problème de l'origine de l'âme de la patristique à la solution thomiste," *Recherches de Théologie Ancienne et Médiévale* 31 (1964): 175–229. This view was of course well known in the Middle Ages, but by the tenth century Gunzo suggests that only a very foolish person would accept Pythagoras's doctrine of metempsychosis. See Gunzo's *Epistola ad Augienses*, 8.35.22.

119. On these two views, see especially A. Michel, "Traducianisme," *Dictionnaire de Théologie Catholique* 15: 1351–1366. For a general discussion of original sin, creationism and traducianism in the early Church, see J.N.D. Kelly, *Early Christian Doctrines*, 5th ed. rev. (New York: Harper and Row, 1978): 174–183; 344–374.

Daly suggests that Augustine may have vacillated here because of his concept of a seminal nature of humankind. See Gabriel Daly, "Theological Models in the Doctrine of Original Sin," *Heythrop Journal* 13 (1972): 127.

120. Augustine, *Epistle* 166.3.8, PL 33: 723. Whether this is actually Jerome's view is unclear. See Gerard O'Daly, *Augustine's Philosophy of Mind* (London: Duckworth, 1987), 19.

121. Augustine, *Epistle* 190.15, PL 33: 862. "Tamquam lucerna de lucerna accendatur et sine detrimento alterius alter inde ignis existat, sic anima de anima parentis fiat in prole, vel traducatur in prolem."

122. Augustine, *Epistle* 166.8.26, PL 33:731.

123. Augustine, *Epistle* 167.1.2, PL 33: 733. "Cum quidem ruisset in puteum, ubi aqua tanta erat, ut eum magis exciperet ne moreretur, quam suffocaret ne loqueretur; accessit alius, et eo viso admirans ait: Quomodo huc cecidisti? At ille: Obsecro, inquit, cogita quomodo hinc me liberes; non quomodo huc ceciderim, queras." For this translation, I have relied upon Augustine's *Letters, IV (165–203)*, trans. Sr. Wilfrid Parsons, The Fathers of the Church, vol. 12 (Washington, DC: Catholic University of America Press, 1964), 33.

124. Marcrobius defends the view that there is a single World-Soul which is the source for all individual souls. See his *Commentarii in Somnium Scipionis* 1.6.20, ed. Jacob Willis (Leipzig: Teubner, 1970). During the last quarter of the eleventh century, Manegold of Lautenbach complained of those who received this doctrine favorably. See the *Liber Magistri Manigaldi contra Wolfelmum Coloniensem*, ed. Wilfried Hartmann, MGH, Quellen 8 (Weimar: Bohlau, 1972), 1–2. For a study of this work, see Hartmann's "Manegold von Lautenbach und die Anfänge der Frühscholastik," *Deutsches Archiv für Erforschung des Mittelalters* 26 (1970): 47–149.

125. Cassiodorus, *De anima* (PL 70: 1279–1308). See especially chapter 7, "De origine animae," PL 70: 1292–93.

126. Prudentius, *Carmen Apotheosis*, in his *Works*, ed. and trans. H.J. Thompson (2 vols.; Cambridge, MA: Harvard University Press, 1949), 1: lns. 780–990.

127. *Tractatus de anima* 2 (PL 110: 1112C). Rabanus Maurus does not share Augustine's hesitancy, but declares himself strongly in favor of creationism.

128. *Liber contra objectiones Fredegisi abbatis*, 14 (PL 104: 168).

129. For additional citations, see especially Michel, "Traducianisme," 1355–1358.

130. *Ad Everardum monachum, de tribus quaestionibus*, 4, in *Opera omnia*, ed. Robert-Henri Bautier et al. (Paris: Éditions du Centre National de la Recherche Scientifique, 1972),134–151.

131. *Deflorationes SS. Patrum*, 2: *De origine animae* (PL 157: 1161–62).

132. *Epistola ad G. Andegavensem* (PL 166: 833–36).

133. Perhaps the clearest example is Aelred of Rievaulx. See his *Dialogus de anima* in *Opera omnia*, ed. A. Hoste and C.H. Talbot, CCCM 1 (Turnhout: Brepols, 1971), 685–754. This text, the *Dialogue on the Soul*, has been translated by C.H. Talbot for the Cistercian Fathers Series, no. 22 (Kalamazoo, MI: Cistercian Publications, 1981).

134. *Sententiae*, 18.8; 31.2.

135. *Sententiarum libri octo*, 2.8 (PL 186: 731A).

136. *De natura et origine animae*, tr. 1, c. 3 (p. 9, ln. 5). For a relevant discussion of the impact of Aristotelian materials on thirteenth century discussions of the origin of the soul, cf. Pamela M. Huby, "Soul, Life, Sense, Intellect: Some Thirteenth-Century Problems," in *The Human Embryo: Aristotle and the Arabic and European Traditions*, ed. G.R. Dunstan (Exeter: University of Exeter Press, 1990), 113–122.

137. For Thomas's view, see *De potentia*, q. iii, art. 9. For a discussion, see Jean-Marie Dubois, "Transmission et rémission du péché originel. Genèse de la réflexion théologique de saint Thomas d'Aquin," *Revue des Études Augustiniennes* 29 (1983): 283–311.

138. See Michel, "Traducianisme," 1358.

139. For a good discussion of the activities of one of Odo's contemporaries, Constantine the African, as a translator of Arabic medical and scientific treatises, see Monica H. Green, "Constantinus Africanus and the Conflict between Religion and Science," in *The Human Embryo: Aristotle and the Arabic and European Traditions*, 47–69; and Joan Cadden, *Meanings of Sex Difference in the Middle Ages* (Cambridge: Cambridge University Press, 1993), 54–70. Constantine was a Benedictine monk at Monte Cassino during the latter half of the eleventh century. In his work one can find new doctrines that will affect medieval notions of conception, embryology, and human development. One finds little or no evidence, however, that Odo was familiar with this material. Rather, his approach remains tied to traditional philo-sophical and theological authorities.

140. See especially *De conceptu virginali et originali peccato*, 23 (*Opera omnia* 2: 165).

141. Eadmer, *The Life of St. Anselm*, ed. R.W. Southern (London: T. Nelson, 1962), 142. "Et quidem si voluntas ejus in hoc est. voluntati ejus libens parebo. Verum si [Deus] mallet me adhuc inter vos saltem tam diu manere, donec quae-stionem quam de origine animae mente revolvo absolvere possem. gratanter ac-ciperem, eo quod nescio utrum aliquis eam me defuncto sit soluturus."

142. For this claim, see also J.M. da Cruz Pontes, "Le problème de l'origine de l'âme," 191.

143. For a discussion of Odo's position, see my "Odo of Tournai's *De peccato originali* and the Problem of Original Sin," in *Medieval Philosophy and Theology* 1 (1991): 18–38.

144. Gregory's opinion (found in his *Epistola* 9, 52, PL 77: 989) is quoted later by Odorannus of Sens. See his *Ad Everardum monachum, de tribus quaestionibus*, 4, p. 135.

145. For the dating of Anselm's work, see Hopkins, *Anselm of Canterbury*, 3: 259, n. 1.

146. Julius Gross provides no evidence to support his claim. See his *Geschichte des Erbsündendogmas*, vol. 3: *Entwicklungsgeschichte des Erbsündendogmas im Zeitalter der Scholastik (12.–15. Jahrhundert)* (Basel and Munich: Ernst Reinhart Verlag, 1971), 28. It is true that (D) has the *incipit*, "Incipit liber domni Odonis cameracen-sis episcopi de originali peccato" ("Here begins the book on original sin of Lord Odo, Bishop of Cambrai . . .") but it is clear that this line was added later, as were chapter headings and divisions (see above, pp. 33–34). It hardly provides evidence

that the work was written during Odo's episcopacy. Rather, it is likely that the copyist later provided Odo's episcopal title. By contrast in the *incipit* to the *Disputation* Odo identifies himself with his episcopal title.

147. For Anselm's discussion of original justice and original sin, see especially *De conceptu virginali et originali peccato*, 1–2 (*Opera omnia* 2: 140–142). For a good discussion, see A. Michel, "Justice originelle," *Dictionnaire de Théologie Catholique* 8: 2020–2042. Some of the older literature on Anselm's understanding of original justice remains useful. See John R. Sheets, "Justice in the Moral Thought of St. Anselm," *Modern Schoolman* 25(1948): 132–139; Raymond M. Martin, "La question du péché originel dans Saint Anselme (1099–1100)," *Revue des Sciences Philosophiques et Théologiques* 5 (1911): 735–749; François de Paule Blachère, "La péché originel d'après Saint Anselme," *Revue Augustinienne* 6 (1905): 241–255; and P.J. Toner, "St. Anselm's Definition of Original Sin," *Irish Theological Quarterly* 3 (1908): 425–436. For Odo's definition of original justice, see *De peccato originali* (PL 160: 1075–76).

148. For Odo's treatment of the Incarnation and Atonement, see his *Disputatio contra Judaeum Leonem nomine de adventu Christi filii Dei* (PL 160: 1101–1112), translated for this volume.

149. See, for example, Johann Eduard Erdmann, *A History of Philosophy*, trans. Williston S. Hough (2 vols.; London and New York: Macmillan Co., 1910), 1: 159.1; Odon Lottin, *Psychologie et morale aux XIIe et XIIIe siècles* (Louvain: Abbaye du Mont César, 1954), 4:167–68; D.E. De Clerck, "Questions de sotériologie médiévale," *Recherches de Théologie Médiévale* 13(1946): 160; and Henri Rondet, *Le péché originel dans la tradition patristique et théologique* (Paris: Fayard, 1967), 185. Similarly, Grabmann describes Odo as a member of Anselm's school of thought, at least in his teaching on original sin. See Martin Grabmann, *Die Geschichte der scholastischen Methode* (Berlin: Akademie-Verlag, 1956), 2:156. Fairweather repeats this claim in his *A Scholastic Miscellany: Anselm to Ockham* (Philadelphia: Westminster Press, 1956), 58.

150. Maurice de Wulf seems to imply as much in his treatment of Odo's work. See his *Histoire de la philosophie médiévale*, 6th ed. (Louvain: Institut Superieur de Philosophie, 1934), 1:172.

151. For a discussion of Anselm's view, see Jasper Hopkins, *A Companion to the Study of St. Anselm* (Minneapolis: University of Minnesota Press, 1972), 206–210. Gilbert Crispin's work, *De anima*, found in British Library MS Add. 8166, fols. 37–39, has recently been published in *The Works of Gilbert Crispin Abbot of Westminster*, ed. Anna Sapir Abulafia and G.R. Evans (London: Oxford University Press, 1989), 157–164. For his apparent defense of traducianism, see especially *De anima* 16, 159.

152. See Émile Amann, "Odo de Cambrai," *Dictionnaire de Théologie Catholique* 11: 933–34. For extensive discussion of Odo's *De peccato originali*, see F. Labis, "Le bienheureaux Odon, Évêque de Cambrai," *Revue Catholique de Louvain* 8 (1856): 453–460, 519–526; 574–585; and Blaise Hauréau, *Histoire de la philosophie scolastique* (Paris: Durand et Pedone-Lauriel, 1872), 1: 296–309. Some interpreters seem to misunderstand Odo's position and wrongly place him among the traducianists. See, for example, C.H. Talbot's introduction to Aelred of Rievaulx's *Dialogue on the Soul*, 18.

153. See Tertullian's *De anima*, 5.

154. See *De peccato originali*, 2, PL 160: 1085D.

155. "nam si solum corpus ab Adam habeo, animam vero non ab Adam, sed a solo Deo, cum peccatum in anima tantum sit, et non in corpore, quomodo dicor in Adam pecasse?" *De peccato originali*, 2, PL 160: 1078C.

156. See K.M. Purday, "Berengar and the Use of the Word *Substantia*," *Downside Review* 91 (1973): 101–110.

157. See his *Expositio*, PL 160: 1059C–D and 1063B for his use of *substantia, res, species, forma*, and *figura*.

158. This is the title under which this text appears in printed editions and in late medieval manuscripts (for example, Harvard University MS Judaica 16). The oldest manuscripts available, however, do not attest to this title. The twelfth-century copy in (D) identifies this work with only the short title *De adventu Christi.* Although the longer title is more descriptive, the reader should not assume that it is Odo's, or that it suggests any formal relationship to the genre of disputed questions in the schools. On these, see Bernardo C. Bazàn, *Les questions disputées*, in *Les questions disputées et les questions quodlibétiques dans les facultés de théologie, de droit et de médicine*, fasc 44–45, Typologie des Sources du Moyen Âge Occidental (Turnhout: Brepols, 1985), 21–149.

159. Regrettably, Peter Browe does not list Odo's work in his catalogue of this literary genre. His discussion of the aim and content of such works, however, remains valuable. See Peter Browe, *Die Judenmission im Mittelalter und die Päpste*, Miscellanea Historiae Pontificiae, 6(Rome, 1973), 99–121.

160. Ceillier also identifies Acard as the recipient of this letter, but acknowledges that some late medieval historians identified the recipient as a monk named Wolbodon, suggesting the possibility of another manuscript tradition. See Rémy Ceillier, *Histoire Générale des Auteurs Sacrés et Ecclésiastiques* (Paris: L. Vives, 1858–1863), 14/1: 75.

161. Perhaps the same sermon that inspired Herman to write a treatise on the Incarnation. See "Monumenta Historiae Tornacensis," in MGH, SS, 14, 268, 35–37; 269, 9–19.

162. "cum Pictavos irem ad consilium, quia die quam Silvanectis ipsum negotium congruenter, adjuvante Deo, contra Judaeum quemdam fueram exsecutus, visum est mihi congruum hanc quaestionem exsequi more dialogi, ut Judaeus queasivit et ego respondi" (PL 160: 1103A).

163. See "Senlis," *Encyclopaedia Judaica* 14: 1161.

164. In this it is distinguished from many other anti-Jewish polemics. Regarding other texts within this genre from the eleventh century, Anna Sapir Abulafia describes such disputations as a kind of ritualized aggression modeled after warfare. She adds that "Their mode of discussion conforms with the conventions of their times. One could even propound that a polite tone of voice should have surprised us more than the rude one we encounter [here]." See her "A Eleventh-Century Exchange of Letters Between a Christian and a Jew," *Journal of Medieval History* 7(1981), 164. The "courteous" tone of Odo's dialogue invites comment from Gilbert Dahan as well. See his *Les intellectuels chrétiens et les juifs au moyen âge* (Paris: Éditions du Cerf, 1990), 417.

165. This is an important feature in the development of Jewish-Christian

debate at the beginning of the twelfth century. See Anna Sapir Abulafia, "Jewish-Christian Disputations and the Twelfth-Century Renaissance," *Journal of Medieval History* 15 (1989): 105–125.

166. Dahan notes that even though the dialogue may itself be a fictional device, it nevertheless seems to have been occasioned by a real encounter with a Jew as Odo made his way to Poitiers. See his *Les intellectuels chrétiens et les juifs au moyen âge*, 342. The real name of the Jew Odo encountered is not known, but in the dialogue he is given the name Leo. This may reflect the fact that Leo is sometimes a title applied to Jews in a conventional sense, designating a member of the community of Judah. See "Titles of Nobility," *Encyclopedia Judaica* 15: 1165–66.

167. The argument continues over the claim introduced more than a century ago by Harnack, namely that most Christian-Jewish dialogues are not records of actual encounters between Jews and Christians so much as they are Christian writings intended for use within the community to strengthen Christian faith. Harnack's point of view is reflected in Amos B. Hulen's "The 'Dialogues with the Jews' as Sources for the Early Jewish Argument Against Christianity," *Journal of Biblical Literature* 5 (1932): 58–70. At stake is not only the usefulness of such "dialogues" as historical documents, but also opinion regarding the possibility of continuing Jewish-Christian encounters. Rosemary Radford Ruether, for example, regards these "dialogues" as having little historical value. Rather, they represent a product of the Christian imagination interested in stigmatizing the religious "other." See her *Faith and Fratricide: The Theological Roots of Anti-Semitism* (New York: Seabury Press, 1974), chapter 3. For a good survey of the various positions and the literature here, see David Rokéah, "The Church Fathers and the Jews in Writings Designed for Internal and External Use," in *Antisemitism Through the Ages*, ed. Shmuel Almog (Oxford: Pergamon Press, 1988), 39–70.

168. For a survey of such polemical treatises, Peter Browe's *Die Judenmission im Mittelalter und die Päpste* remains useful.

169. Gilbert Dahan, *Les intellectuels chrétiens et les juifs au moyen âge*, 470.

170. Daniel Lasker discusses what may be the earliest example in his *"Qiṣṣat Mujādalat al-Usquf and Nestor Ha-Komer. The Earliest Arabic and Hebrew Jewish anti-Christian Polemics,"* in *Genizah Research After Ninety Years: The Case of Judeo-Arabic*, ed. J. Blau and S.C. Reif (Cambridge: Cambridge University Press, 1992), 112–118.

171. Bernhard Blumenkranz, "Jüdische und christliche Konvertiten im jüdische-christlichen Religionsgespräch des Mittelalters," in *Judentum im Mittelalter: Beiträge zum christlich-jüdischen Gespräch*, ed. Paul Wilpert and Willehad Paul Eckert, Miscellanea Mediaevalia 4 (Berlin: De Gruyter, 1966), 264–282.

172. For additional information on Obadiah and Andreas, see also "Obadiah the Norman Proselyte," *Encyclopaedia Judaica* 12: 1306–1308.

173. As they were, for example, in Lambert's *Liber Floridus*, completed about 1120. On this work, see Max Manitius, *Geschichte der lateinische Literatur des Mittelalters* (3 vols.; Munich: C.H. Beck, 1911–1931), 3:242–43.

174. *Cur Deus Homo* was probably completed about 1098. Odo's text was probably written in 1105 or 1106.

175. Some, it is true, have identified Anselm's interlocutor, Boso, as a common

spokesperson for Jews and Muslims, that is, non-believers. Cf. René Roques, "La méthode de Saint Anselme dans le 'Cur Deus Homo'," *Aquinas. Ephemerides Thomisticae* 5 (1962): 3–57. Nevertheless, the formal difference between the two treatises remains.

176. Cf. *Cur Deus Homo*, 1.11.

177. See W.F. Ewbank, "Anselm, on Sin and Atonement," *Church Quarterly Review* 146 (1948): 61–67.

178. The prologue to this letter is found in the "Monumenta Historiae Tornacensis," in MGH, SS, 14, 267.

179. For an edition and translation, see the unpublished thesis of Paul Naedenoen, "Odon de Cambrai: Traité sur le canon de la Messe."

180. *Maxima bibliotheca veterum patrum*, ed. Maguerin de la Bigne (27 vols.; Cologne: 1577), 21: 227–241 (*De peccato originali*) and 241–244 (*Disputatio contra Judaeum*).

181. See *Expositio*, PL 1060: 1070D.

182. Although catalogues suggest that (T) contains *De peccato originali*, the very helpful staff at the Centre National de la Recherche Scientifique, Institut de Recherche et d'Histoire des Textes (in Paris) verified that in fact this manuscript contains *only* Odo's *Disputatio contra Judaeum*. The catalogues are in error.

183. See Naedenoen, "Odon de Cambrai: Traité sur le Canon de la Messe," cxxxiv.

On Original Sin (De peccato originali)

1. Although Odo does not identify the orthodox in this treatise, elsewhere he introduces a definition that is quite traditional. In his *Expositio in canonem missae*, written sometime after A.D. 1105, he identifies the orthodox as simply those who are distinguished by both their doctrine and their manner of living. See *Expositio*, PL 160: 1056B.

2. For the importance of this remark for dating this composition, see above, p. 26. Odo's protestations here are quite traditional, and may be nothing more than a literary device. A similar protest is found in the preface to his *Expositio in canonem missae*, PL 160: 1053–54.

3. For a nearly contemporary treatment of this text, and the problems it raised, cf. Peter Damian's *De divina omnipotentia*, 3, 597C, ed. André Cantin, *Lettre sur la toute-puissance divine* (Paris: Éditions du Cerf, 1972), 392.

4. But cf. Lev. 15: 2.

5. One may compare Odo's remarks here to Augustine's description of the human soul as a rational substance created by God and equipped to rule the body. See his *De quantitate animae*, 13, translated in Wippel and Wolter, *Medieval Philosophy from St. Augustine to Nicholas of Cusa*, 61.

6. Reading, "Sic instituit deus, et ideo male operando operarii mali non sumus" (D) for "operarii mali non sumus" (M).

7. Adding "nec male agendo mali sumus" (D) before "quia non agimus malum nostrum" (M).

8. Odo makes it clear below that this is the error of the Manichaeans.

9. The Manichaeans, a heretical sect St. Augustine attacked most vehemently in the early Church, insisted upon distinct and co-eternal principles of good and evil in order to explain their continuing conflict in the world. Odo makes this explicit at *De peccato originali* 1, PL 160: 1075D. See above, p. 45. Augustine, who was himself associated with the Manichaeans before his conversion, explains he too had thus concluded that evil must be a substance or essence in its own right. See his *Confessions* 15.24. In the Middle Ages "manichaean" had become a general term of opprobrium to describe a variety of theological errors. Thus in the early eleventh century Bishop Gerard of Cambrai reports the condemnation of a group of "manichaeans" at the Council of Arras (A.D. 1025). See *Epistola Gerardi Acta Synodi Atrebatensis in Manichaeos*, 8 and 9, PL 142: 1296C and 1298–99. On the date of this council, see Jeffrey Burton Russell, "A propos du synode d'Arras, en 1025," *Revue d'Histoire Ecclésiastique* 57(1962): 66–87. Similarly, another group of "manichaeans" is condemned at Orléans about A.D. 1015. See Jeffrey Burton Russell, *Dissent and Reform in the Early Middle Ages* (Berkeley and Los Angeles: University of California Press, 1965), 34–35.

10. It is comforting to translate *singularia* here as "individuals," according to contemporary usage, since he is comparing the members of a species with the species itself. But Odo does use the term *singularis* in a more technical sense, which may sometimes elude us, based upon his realist metaphysics. Thus one may have an individual of a species — the concrete individual — and an individual or singular universal, which is not at all concrete. For this distinction, see especially *De peccato originali*, 2, PL 160: 1080B–C.

11. Reading "nomen omne significativum est alicujus ad placitum" (D) for "nomen omne significativum est ad placitum" (M).

12. Reading "si nec Latinus, ut dicit" (D) for "Sic nec Latinus" (M).

13. Cf. Anselm, *De casu diaboli*, 10 (*Opera omnia* 1:247).

14. "Talibus rationibus defendunt manichei malum aliquid esse et essentiam habere, et igitur inde coguntur heresim facere et instruere quendam omnium malorum conditorem." This passage appears in (D) but not in (M).

15. For the very traditional notion that evil is a privation of good, see especially Augustine, *Confessions* 4.15.24, 5.10.20, and 7.12.18.

16. Cf. Aristotle, *Categories* 11b18–19.

17. Namely, privation and possession. Cf. Martianus Capella, *The Marriage of Philology and Mercury*, 4.386. I have used the translation of William Harris Stahl and E.L. Burge, volume 2 of *Martianus Capella and the Seven Liberal Arts* (New York: Columbia University Press, 1977), 131.

18. Cf. Anselm, *De conceptu virginali et originali peccato*, 5 (*Opera omnia* 2: 146–47).

19. That is, the absent attribute or property. For example, a blind person lacking sight suggests a case of privation because sight naturally ought to exist in the person. An animal that does not naturally enjoy sight, however, cannot be said to be deprived of it and therefore this would not constitute an example of privation. We cannot speak of privation, then, every time the "privative" — in this instance, sight — is absent.

20. The Latin, "sine privati debito," suggests the "debt" that the privation owes for its "existence" to that reality upon which it depends.

21. Reading "Quod mala non habent genera vel species" (D) for "Quod mala non habent species generales" (M).

22. Reading "econverso tamen ex ipsis negatis similitudinem generum sumunt et specierum imitationem, non veritatem" (D) for "econverso tamen ex ipsis negatis similitudinem generum sumunt et specierum mutationem vel veritatem" (M).

23. *in ante praedicamentis*, a technical term referring to the first part of the *Categories*. For Boethius's understanding of *praedicamenta*, see his *De trinitate* 4.1. Odo's point is that not-animal can act like a species of not-man, since everything that is not an animal is also not a man. When expressed positively, however, animal is not a species of man, but rather man is a species of animal, so that it is not true that everything that is an animal is also a man. I have been unable to locate the passage Odo refers to in the works of Boethius.

24. Reading "imitatio" (D) for "mutatio" (M).

25. Boethius may be Odo's source for this discussion of privations. In his *In Ciceronis Topica* he notes that

> According to Cicero, privating contraries . . . have as a prefix a part of speech whose addition to a word nearly always removes something. This is the prefix "in," for the addition of this syllable usually takes away something of the force that a thing would have had if it had not had "in" prefixed, such as "humanity" and "inhumanity," (for when "in" is prefixed, that of which it is said is deprived of humanity), or "dignity" and "indignity." Cicero maintains that only those words in which the syllable "in" is prefixed are privating contraries; indeed, according to Cicero, the nature of privating contraries is defined by the expression of this syllable. But from the Peripatetics we have received the idea that privations are expressed sometimes by simple names and sometimes with privative syllables — by simple names, as, for example, "blindness" and with privative syllables, as, for example, "indignity" and "inhumanity."

For this translation, see *Boethius's In Ciceronis Topica*, trans. Eleonore Stump (Ithaca, NY: Cornell University Press, 1988), 120. For the Latin text, see PL 64: 1119–20.

26. For Alcuin and other Carolingian dialecticians, the negation not-man is an "infinite" noun. That is, it does not designate what something is, but rather the infinite number of things it is not. Odo certainly understands this as well, even though he does not employ their terminology. For Alcuin's explanation, see his *De dialectica*, 12, PL 101: 964D.

27. I have found no good English equivalent for *habitus*. It refers to the presence of an attribute in a subject, where it ought to be present, and thus stands opposed to a privation. Although sometimes rendered "condition," this seems to me no more helpful than "possession." From this point on, however, I shall use the Latin *habitus* in the text in order to help avoid confusion.

28. Or, perhaps, "own being."

29. Odo seems to be thinking again of the parable of the hidden talents. See the prologue to *On Original Sin*, p. 39.

30. Cf. Anselm, *De casu diaboli*, 9 (*Opera omnia* 1: 246).

31. Anselm's students ask the same question. See his *De conceptu virginali et originali peccato*, 6 (*Opera omnia* 2: 147); cf. Honorius, *Elucidarium* 2.3, in *L'Elucidiarium et les lucidaires*, ed. Yves Lefèvre, Bibliothèque des Écoles Françaises d'Athènes et de Rome, 124 (Paris: 1954), 405.

32. Not only because justice is absent from the soul, but because it is missing from where it ought to be. Justice, as one of the four primary philosophical virtues of the soul—justice, courage, temperance, and prudence—is a *habitus* of the soul which cannot be lost unwillingly. Its absence, then, represents a privation resulting from a defection of the will. Cf.Rabanus Maurus, *Tractatus de anima*, 6, PL 110: 115.

33. Virgil, *Bucolics*, eclog. 3, 108. Odo's meaning seems to be "Have it your own way!"

34. "Relation"—*ad aliquid*—is identified as a category in the Ps. Augustinian *Ten Categories*, but opposites, for example, are distinguished from relation, including the example Odo employs here, namely injustice. For the text, see the *Categoriae decem* 108–110 in *Aristoteles Latinus* 1.1–5, 158.

35. For one source of the view that every predicate corresponds to an existent nature, see Fredigisus of Tours's *De nihil et tenebris*, PL 105: 752C. This text is translated in *Medieval Philosophy from St. Augustine to Nicholas of Cusa*, 104–108. For a discussion of Fredigisus's text, and a corrected edition, see Francesco Corvino, "Il 'de nihilo et tenebris' di Fredegiso di Tours," *Revista Critica di Storia della Filosofia* 47(1956): 273–286. For his contribution to pre-Scholastic philosophy, see John Marenbon's *From the Circle of Alcuin to the School of Auxerre*, 62–66. Also see Marcia L. Colish, "Carolingian Debates over *Nihil* and *Tenebrae*: A Study in Theological Method," *Speculum* 59/4(1984): 757–795.

36. Reading "Alioquin de eo quod non est aliquid dici non potest. Certe potest per consuetudinem, potest per necessitatem. Saepe enim necesse nobis est loqui de his quae non sunt" (D) for "Alioquin de eo quod non est aliquid dici potest. Certe non potest per consuetudinem, potest per necessitatem. Neque enim necesse nobis loqui de his quae non sumt" (M). Odo's point is that sometimes it becomes necessary to speak of things that do not exist, but that we can only do so by appropriating a name for such non-existents from things which do exist and have their own proper names. So, for example, injustice does not exist, so to speak of injustice we must appropriate a name from that which does, namely justice. The "name" injustice, however, cannot be rooted in a real or existent nature. It must then be the product of a linguistic convention and not grounded in a *nature*, as one should find with a real object. It goes well beyond my purpose here to discuss medieval debates over whether language is natural or the product of convention. For some discussion of this problem for the Christian tradition, see my "*Lingua Dei, lingua hominis*: Sacred Language and Medieval Texts," *Viator* 21(1990): 57–58.

37. Odo remains fairly consistent in using *figura* to refer to the sensible form of a material body and *forma* to refer to the form of an incorporeal substance. "Figure" does not convey quite the same sense in English. According to the context, I shall sometimes use "image," "figure," or "shape" to describe the form of a material body in order to preserve Odo's distinction—one that can be found in Boethius's

Philosophiae consolationis 5.4.85, and his *In Isagogen Porphyrii Commenta*, editionis primae 2.6 and editionis secundae, 4.11 as well. This sense of *figura* as the sensible shape or appearance of a thing is also evident in Odo's description of the consecrated host on the altar. Although the body of Christ present there is one substance, it appears in as many *figurae* as there are offerings. See his *Expositio in canonem missae* PL 160: 1068D.

38. Cf. Anselm, *Monologion*, 11 (*Opera omnia* 1:26).

39. Horace, *Ars poetica*, 9.10.

40. Or, perhaps, "concept."

41. Or, reading "peccatorem" (D) for "executorem" (M), "you have made yourself a sinner."

42. Reading "originalis" (D) for "originatis" (M).

43. Odo does not suggest that the orthodox position has been established by conciliar decree. Yet, by the time that *De peccato originali* was written, Odo could be confident that many orthodox theologians held this view. One-hundred-fifty years earlier, Ratramnus had simply declared that the anti-traducianist position is the faith of the Catholic Church. See Ratramnus of Corbie, *Liber de anima ad Odonem Bellovacensem*, ed. D.C. Lambot, Analecta Mediaevalia Namurcensia, 2 (Namur: Centre d'Études Médiévales, 1951), 134.20. Moreover, Odo's near contemporary, Rupert of Deutz, confirms that it is the "single opinion of all the orthodox [believers]" that "souls do not descend from a root-stock." *De trinitate et operibus ejus: In Gen.* 2.21, PL 167: 267B.

44. Although Odo does not say so here, others had clearly stigmatized traducianism as a doctrine that undermines the notion of original sin. Cf. Rabanus Maurus, *Tractatus de anima*, 2, PL 110: 1112C.

45. That is, the orthodox doctrine.

46. In a somewhat different context, the Carolingian theologian Alcuin felt compelled to respond to the objection that, if God rested on the seventh day, he could not be responsible for creating the diversity of tongues at Babel. In an effort to blunt this objection, Alcuin answers that the division of tongues is not a new creation, but only a division of already existent linguistic forms into diverse genera. See his *Interrogationes et Responsiones in Genesim*, q. 151, PL 100: 534A.

47. Again, it seems, the orthodox party.

48. The same opinion is expressed by Odo's contemporary, Hugh of Ribemont. Hugh also responds to those who complain that the view that new souls are created daily contradicts the sense of Gen. 2: 2. Hugh agrees that all things [or species] were created in the beginning and then God rested. But subsequently *individuals* come into existence through their own proper act or matter. Souls however are created new daily *ex nihilo*, and do not descend from a root-stock. *Epistola ad G. Andegavensem*, PL 166: 835A.

49. For another appeal to Jn. 5: 17 with the same theological intent, see Werner of St. Blaise, *Deflorationes SS. Patrum*, 2, PL 157: 1161C; Honorius, *Elucidarium* 2.35.

50. This passage was utilized both in support of the claim that God creates new souls for individual bodies and in support of the claim that there is some pre-existent incorporeal matter or root-stock from which souls descend to bodies. See the dispute between the Carolingian theologian Agobard of Lyon and Fredigisus of

Tours in Agobard's *Contra objectiones Fredigi abbatis*, 14, PL 104: 169B. Agobard shares Odo's conclusion, however, that *orthodox* doctors of the Church agree that the soul is created by God at the same moment that the body is created (PL 104: 169D).

51. While the phrase "secundum hos" may be ambiguous, the context suggests that Odo is speaking of the orthodox party.

52. This same question is attributed by Aelred of Rievaulx about the middle of the twelfth century, in almost identical language, to "heretics" who attack original sin and the necessity of infant baptism because of alleged difficulties with creationism. Clearly their conclusion (Albigensians?) was that we have *not* sinned in Adam. The difficulties attached to the two alternatives — creationism or traducianism — lead Aelred to claim that the problem is an insoluble one. See his *Dialogus de anima* 1.59.742–757, p. 703.

53. Or: "in which *my* sin is" reading "in quam meum peccatum" (D) for "in qua peccatum" (M).

54. Reading "Quando peccavit, quia corpus meum tunc in ipso erat" (D) for "Quando peccavit in corpus meum tunc in ipso erat" (M). Odo does accept that our bodies descend directly from Adam, in whom all bodies were potentially present at creation, much as the second generation is "genetically" present in the parent generation. This notion of direct descent is implicit earlier in this section when Odo remarks that "whatever corporeal things are created each day arise from the seeds of the first creation, and no corporeal thing may exist that does not descend from this first beginning." Although Odo does not use the Augustinian terminology, he may have in mind Augustine's seminal reasons (*rationales seminales*) to explain not only the rule according to which later generations of humans are produced from the first, but also to explain the sense in which all are "present" (potentially, as effects) in the first man as cause. The nature of their presence in the first man was, however, subject to controversy. Anselm complains of those critics who regarded this existence in the first man, as cause of men (and women) coming later, as a perfectly *vacuous* existence, not properly called existence at all. Anselm, however, takes up a position very similar to Odo's. See Anselm's *De conceptu virginali et originali peccato*, 23.

55. These difficulties following upon the notion that the soul is created ex nihilo are profound, and clearly entered into religious polemics in the Middle Ages. As Joel Rembaum shows, Jewish writers used these very points to attack the orthodox notion of original sin. See Rembaum's "Medieval Jewish Criticism of the Christian Doctrine of Original Sin," *Association for Jewish Studies* 7–8 (1982–83): 369.

56. That is, an answer to the question "What is it?" that provides only the genus is inadequate for it is too abstract and remote from the object. Cf. Ps. Augustine's *Ten Categories* 59, p. 146 and Boethius's translation of the *Categories* 2b5, in *Aristoteles Latinus* 1.1–5: *Categoriae vel Praedicamenta*, p. 8. But the species does, for Odo, denote the substance of the thing, indicating again Odo's realist position with respect to universals. As we see below, *individuals* have nothing more than species with respect to substance. Thus in answer to the question "What is it?" both answers — "It is a man" and "It is Peter" — seem to suffice for him. This may be quite different than the position one finds expressed in Martianus Capella, for example, where the individual is identified as primary substance and the species or genus as

secondary substance, followed by the conclusion that "primary substance is more truly substance than is secondary substance; for primary substance more directly identifies the thing." *The Marriage of Philology and Mercury*, 4.365, p. 122.

57. Reading "individua vero nihil habent substantialiter plus quam species, nec aliud sunt substantialiter quam species. Non est enim substantialiter aliud Petrus quam homo" (D) for "individuo vero nihil habent substantialiter plus quam species, nec aliud sunt substantialiter, aliud Petrus quam homo" (M).

58. Individuals are accidental to the species in the sense that the species is unaffected and unchanged by the coming-to-be or the destruction of this individual or that, so long as at least *one* individual remains. Unlike individuals, then, the species cannot pass out of existence. The possibility that *all* individuals of a species should be destroyed (and the species with it) was never envisioned by Odo.

59. "specialis natura."

60. Reading "Species etiamsi de uno solo dicitur, de pluribus dici potest. Species etiamsi de uno solo dicatur, universalis est. Individuum vero nonnisi singulare est" (D) for "Species etiamsi de uno solo dicitur, universalis est; individuum vero nonnisi singulare est" (M).

61. On the disparity between sense and reason, see Odo's *Disputatio contra Judaeum Leonem nomine de adventu Christi filii Dei*, p. 95–96 in the present volume.

62. The nature of this division would appear to be both logical and ontological. The universal species nature, the human soul, is "divided" when individual souls are formed for individual bodies. But this type of division is not identical for Odo to the division affirmed by the (spiritual) traducianists, who aver that each new soul is divided or separated from its individual parent soul (cf. p. 48 and p. 78 in the present volume). For Odo this division is accomplished whenever a new individual comes into being, but without the separation of a part or seed from a parent soul. The human soul is divided, then, in the sense that the species nature, which is one, can be predicated of many.

63. Anselm employs a similar expression. Cf. Anselm's *De conceptu virginali et originali peccato*, 2 and 10 (*Opera omnia* 2: 141–42, 151–52) and *Cur Deus Homo*, 1.23 (*Opera omnia* 2: 91).

64. Reading "sive persona" (D) for "sine persona" (M).

65. "contractum."

66. Namely, species and genera.

67. R. Van den Broek suggests that it is likely that "even in Hesiod's time it was accepted that only one phoenix existed at a time; just as the rising sun is the same sun that set the day before, it is the same phoenix that dies in decrepitude and is reborn in youthful vigour." *The Myth of the Phoenix According to Classical and Early Christian Traditions* (Leiden: E.J. Brill, 1972), 400. The assumption that there was but one phoenix created some difficulties for medieval logicians, who recognized that in this case the individual is predicated universally. For examples, see De Rijk, *Logica modernorum*, 2/2, p.30.

68. As Peter is in the human race, and the human race is in him.

69. Reading "rationalia" (D) for "rationabilia" (M). For Odo's definition, see Boethius's *Contra Eutychen*, 3.1–5 and 4.8 in *The Theological Tractates*, trans. H.F. Stewart and E.K. Rand, where Boethius identifies person — "an individual sub-

stance of a rational nature" — with the Greek *hypostasis*. For a complaint against the theological constraints that Boethius's definition implied, see Otloh of St. Emmeram's comments in his *Dialogus de tribus quaestionibus*, PL 146: 60B.

70. Boethius adds "nusquam in universalibus persona dici potest." *Contra Eutychen* 2.47, in *The Theological Tractates*, trans. H.F. Stewart and E.K. Rand.

71. Following Ratramnus of Corbie, Odo would agree that every person has a nature, but not every nature a person. The term "person," therefore, cannot be applied to rocks, trees, and other natures lacking reason. A person is a rational substance, and therefore, says Ratramnus, only God, angels, and man can be said to be persons. See Ratramnus, *Liber de anima ad Odonem Bellovacensem*, 62,10.

72. Cf. Martianus Capella, *The Marriage of Philology and Mercury*, 4.388–389, pp. 134–135. Another possible source is Augustine's *De dialectica*, 1.5.6–16, trans. B. Darrell Jackson, ed. Jan Pinborg (Dordrecht and Boston: D. Reidel, 1975).

73. Odo may have in mind here the use of clay masks for *personae dramatis* in the theater.

74. Odo's point is that, despite the contention of grammarians, "person" is a term properly used only for rational individuals. It is used in an extended or tropical sense of other things (the second and third persons of the verb) but this use should not confuse our primary usage, which identifies persons as rational individuals having the property of speech, that is, thought made manifest (and not just vocalized sounds).

75. "similitudinem."

76. This attempts to make sense of an especially terse and difficult passage.

77. Cf. Anselm, *De conceptu virginali et originali peccato*, 2 (*Opera omnia* 2: 141–42)

78. Cf. Odo's *Disputatio contra Judaeum*, p. 90 above.

79. "Reproducing" might be a more familiar contemporary term than "propagating" (Latin, "propagatio, -onis"), but Odo does not merely use this term to describe the generation of the body through sexual intercourse. He also uses it to describe the opinion of the spiritual traducianists, who speak of the propagation of the soul itself. Moreover, in order to preserve Odo's intended analogy to vegetative life, implied by "root-stock" and "seed," I shall use the verb "to propagate." Note too that Augustine uses a related form (Latin, "propago, -inis") in *De libero arbitrio* 3.21.59.200, to describe the view of those I have called spiritual traducianists. Interestingly, he adds that it is impossible to affirm or deny their view, since the question of the origin of the soul is not one the fathers of the church have resolved. Odo is not so cautious.

80. Reading "non conveniunt universalibus" (D) for "tamen conveniunt universalibus" (M).

81. Odo is quite correct that the name Adam usually serves as a collective noun in the Old Testament or Hebrew Bible, referring to humanity as such, even though the Vulgate may obscure this. The passage Odo may have in mind is Gen. 1:26–27. Anselm makes the same point in his *De conceptu virginali et originali peccato*, 9 (*Opera omnia* 2: 149).

82. E.g., immutability. Consequently, *nature* is not at fault as a result of Adam's sin.

83. Reading "potuit habere persona" (D) for "potuit habere personam" (M).

84. Reading "componi dicantur" (D) for "complurimi dicantur" (M).

85. Reading "ad alias personas" (D) for "ab alias personas" (M).

86. Cf. *De peccato originali*, PL 160: 1081C.

87. (D) provides a textual variant that gives the opposite sense—namely that Christ did come from a true marital union—perhaps reflecting contemporary debate. Whether Joseph and Mary enjoyed a true marriage or not was hotly contested at this time. Those theologians who argued that conjugal relations are essential to complete the sacrament of marriage found themselves in some difficulty when discussing the nature of the bond between Joseph and Mary. If conjugal relations are essential to marriage, then it would seem that they could not have been married, properly speaking. This odious conclusion was not lost on Peter Damian, who, in the latter half of the eleventh century, attacked theologians who insisted that sexual relations were a necessary element for marriage. See Damian's *Opusculum* 41, *De tempore celebrandi nuptias*, 4, PL 145: 664D. For a discussion of the developing theology of marriage, see Seamus P. Heaney, *The Developmnt of the Sacramentality of Marriage from Anselm of Laon to Thomas Aquinas*, Catholic University of America Studies in Sacred Theology, 2nd. ser., no. 134 (Washington, DC: Catholic University of America Press, 1963). For a good review of the position of the canonists, see Penny S. Gold, "The Marriage of Mary and Joseph in the Twelfth-Century Ideology of Marriage," in *Sexual Practices and the Medieval Church*, ed. Vern Bullough and James Brundage (Buffalo, NY: Prometheus Books, 1982), 102–117. The marital status of Joseph and Mary was taken up by one of Odo's successors at Tournai toward the middle of the twelfth century, Simon, who, in his *Disputatio* 15, subtly suggests that Joseph and Mary were married, but only "imperfectly." See *Les Disputationes de Simon de Tournai*, ed. Joseph Warichez, Spicilegium Sacrum Lovaniense, Études et Documents 12 (Louvain: 1932), 52–53.

88. Odo frequently reiterates that the Word is born of the Virgin, conceived without a human father and therefore apart from the conditions of human propagation by divine power alone. See his *Expositio in canonem missae*, PL 160: 1064D–1065A.

89. Again, Anselm, makes much the same point. Reproductive capacity was a good when first given to Adam. But it too has become perverted by original sin with the result that each time human beings procreate sin and guilt are passed on. See Anselm's *De conceptu virginali et originali peccato*, 10 (*Opera omnia* 2: 151–152). This helps to explain as well why the Word, conceived without a human father and therefore apart from the natural reproductive act, can be born without sin.

90. Odo is here playing a bit of a word game, difficult to reproduce in translation, when he contrasts the "difficultas pressurarum" present to him with the signs of latent power being expressed ("exprimebantur"), since both "exprimebantur" and "pressurarum" are derived from the verb "premo."

91. Odo uses "contritione" here, translated "contrition." But, again, there is a pun in the Latin, since the root meaning of "contritione" is a "grinding." Just as one grinds grain in order to disclose what is hidden in it, so too Christ was "ground down" in order to reveal his strength.

92. Reading "nascimur" (D) for "nascitur" (M). One might object that this whole passage treats the suffering of Jesus as little more than an example to us of endurance under adverse conditions, lacking the more dramatic and juridical content of Anselm's theory of Atonement. In large measure, however, Odo's failure here is remedied in other texts. In his *Disputatio contra Judaeum* it is made clear that Jesus suffers and dies not merely to provide us with a model of endurance but also to remove from us the weight of original sin. Moreover, in his *Expositio in canonem missae* (PL 160: 1058), Odo explains that when his sacrifice is represented daily on the altar during the Mass, it redeems us from sin and evil by the payment of a price beyond compare.

93. Cf. Anselm, *De conceptu virginali et originali peccato*, 23 (*Opera omnia* 2: 165).

94. Reading "ostensum esse" (D) for "ostensum est" (M).

95. Reading "non secundam eamdem speciem" (M) for "non nisi secundam eamdem speciem" (D). The passage that follows is exceedingly difficult and leads one to speculate that the text here may be corrupt.

96. Latin, "medium."

97. Reading "nullam ibi traducem" (D) for "nullum ibi traducem" (M).

98. Reading "creat" (D) for "ereat" (M).

99. Reading "si nascitur iusta posteritas" (D) for "si nascitur ista posteritas" (M).

100. Reading "Anima stulta, quiesce arguere Conditorem" (D) for "Anima stulta, quisce arguere Creatorem"(M).

101. Odo has already explained in the preceding book that our bodies in some sense already existed in Adam from the very beginning. The soul, however, as we shall see, is created from nothing (qua individual soul) but also comes from an existing soul nature, namely the universal or the species. Consistent with his Christian Platonism, for Odo the forms or natures of all things are eternally existent in the mind or Wisdom of God, although united in one simple nature. Although united in a simple form there, *we* percevie these forms as separate and discrete; although eternal there, they are nevertheless created in time and the world when they come to subsist in created being. See Odo's *Expositio in canonem missae*, PL 160: 1059D–1060B.

102. Reading "sine utraque" (D) for "sive utraque" (M).

103. Reading "Quod unius est" (D) for "Quod unus est" (M).

104. Odo refers here to the traditional Trinitarian formula, that in the Godhead are three Persons — Father, Son, and Holy Spirit — but only one substance of divinity.

105. Odo is describing primary substance which, as Aristotle says in *Categories* 2a14, is not said *of* a subject and is not *in* a subject.

106. "specialis homo."

107. "communis homo."

108. Cf. Augustine, *De libero arbitrio* 3.20.56.189.

109. Reading "ut sit in toto quod superius dictum est de parte" (D) for "ut si in toto quod superius dictum est de parte" (M).

110. Reading "iuste patiendo" (D) for "iuste puniendo" (M).

111. For Odo's understanding of the *bonum palmae*, see especially his *De blasphemia in Spiritum Sanctum*, PL 160: 1117C.

112. Cf. Augustine, *De libero arbitrio*, 3.1.2.9–10. Recall that Odo experienced a sort of conversion when he read the third book of Augustine's *De libero arbitrio*.

113. Reading "aegritudine tristatur" (D) for "aegritudine testatur" (M).

114. Cf. p. 39 in this present volume.

115. (D) adds "cum malo quod non fecit Deus."

116. Elsewhere Odo makes it clear that *man* may forgive sins that *God* may not, and forego punishment while God may not, because of the requirements of divine justice. But then it seems that man may perform some good that God cannot perform. Odo grants this, but adds that even that good comes from God. See *De blasphemia in Spiritum Sanctum*, PL 160: 1114A.

117. Reading "enim a nobis" (D) for "enim a vobis" (M).

118. Reading "creantur cotidie nova individua" (D) for "creantur nova individua" (M).

119. Tullio Gregory understands this to be Odo's final conclusion, supporting a kind of Platonic realism to which Abelard would soon react vigorously. But as the next paragraph indicates, it is a mistake to identify this position as Odo's or as the orthodox position. See Tullio Gregory, *Platonismo medievale*, Studi storici, fasc. 26–28 (Rome: Istituto Storico Italiano per il Medio Evo, 1958), 47–50.

120. Cf. *De peccato originali* 2, PL 160: 1085–1086.

121. Reading "si sola accidentia dicitur" (D) for "si sola accidentia dicuntur" (M).

122. "originaliter."

123. Although it is possible to distinguish between the "whole" and the "totality," as Aristotle does (cf. *Metaphysics*, 5, 24, 1024a), Odo does not seem to do so. Throughout this text, he uses *totum* for "whole," and seems to have no vocabulary to express the distinction found in Aristotle.

124. Odo is using the term "composition" here much like the painter who speakers of a painting's composition, or the musician who writes a new composition.

125. That is, the whole man is the individual man or person, for example Peter.

126. Reading "si tota dicuntur, in individuis suis dicuntur, non per se" (D) for "si tota dicitur, in individuis suis dicuntur per se" (M). Odo discusses this topic earlier at p. 54 above.

127. "sonare."

128. Perhaps Odo is thinking here of Aristotle's division of "quantity" into both discrete and continuous quantity. Even though the universal can be "divided" into species, still it is not said to be a whole except through individuals. See Aristotle, *Categories* 4b6.

129. As number may be divided into its "parts": the odd and the even. But the universal is not composed of parts. It is only *this* number, for example six, that is a sum of other numbers, one, two, and three.

130. Reading "ex genere et differentia" (D) for "ex genere et substantia" (M).

131. "simpliciter."

132. For a definition of "figura," see Bk. 1, p. 46, n. 37 above.

133. adding "siquidem numerus est quantitas" (D).

134. In the section below Odo makes it clear that he rejects the Platonic view that there are several souls in each individual, viz. the nutritive, the sensitive or appetitive, and the rational. Rather, for him soul is a unity, although it has various powers — powers of growth, movement, and reason.

135. Reading "ad invisibilium cognitionem" (D) for "ad invisibilem cognitionem" (M).

136. "species sensuum."

137. That is, a vegetative power.

138. Medieval physicians were very interested in the medical powers or virtues of readily available plants. For a glance at some of the uses of medieval garden plants, see Jerry Stannard, *Selected Medieval Garden Plants and Their Uses* (Lawrence: University of Kansas Press, 1983).

139. Cf. Aristotle, *De anima* 2.2.18–20. Although one can find the same information in Aristotle's work, it must be noted that this work was not available in Latin translation until the thirteenth century.

140. Reading "cum tamen totum ex una vi non constet sola" (D) for "cum tamen totum ex una vi constet sola" (M).

141. Reading "infundatur" (D) for "infundantur" (M).

142. Reading "nunc haec species fiat, nunc illa" (D) for "nunc et species fiat, nunc illa" (M).

143. "Figura." Again, as indicated above on p. 118, n. 37, "figura" can mean "figure," "shape," or sometimes "image," but generally refers to the sensible or material analogue to "form."

144. Reading "Mutata forma alteratur materies in individuis rebus visibiliter, mutata differentia substantiae communis in materie visibili, mutatur specialis natura in eadem visibili materie invisibiliter" (D) for "alteratur materies in individuis rebus visibiliter mutata, differentia substantiae communis in materie visibili, mutatur specialis natura in eadem visibili materie invisibiliter" (M).

145. Reading "Hinc est substantiae specialis individuum, hinc vero partibus suis est totum" (D) for "huic est substantiae specialis, individuum, hinc vero partibus suis est totum" (M).

146. (D) fol. 108r inserts here the first six lines of the section entitled "On Figure," reading "It can be inferred from the preceding that figure (*figura*) becomes the cause of all corporeal things; for without figure even matter cannot be, nor can any species be predicated of individuals in bodies, nor can a material whole be or be composed. Now although corporeal matter can be *conceived* in the mind, it cannot *exist* without figure." This section is repeated at 109r (PL 160: 1097–1098). Since the insertion at 108r appears to have been added later, I have omitted it here and have followed the order present in (M).

147. "Term" (Latin, "finis") here and following should be understood in the sense of the end, utmost limit, or terminus.

148. Reading "praedicandi" and "componendi" (D) for "praedicanda" and "componenda" (M).

149. Reading "medius limes" (D) for "medius" (M).

150. Adding "Extremitas tamen infirma non penitus respuit summam" (D).

151. Or, perhaps, "syllable."

152. Reading "Hoc grammaticus inspicit, qui tamquam pluralem singularem numerum dicit" (D) for "hos grammaticus inspicit, qui tamquam plurale singularem numerum dicit" (M).

153. Cf. Boethius, *De trinitate* 2.28, where Boethius attributes to *forma* the role Odo attributes to *figura*.

154. Reading "aliam speciem corpus ipsum assumit" (D) for "aliam secundam corpus ipsum assumit" (M).

155. "Massa." Odo's point is only that as a human corpse is burned or eaten by worms, its matter assumes a new form and species. What earlier was a man becomes something else.

156. Adding "si in massa non figurantur?" (D).

157. "suis rebus."

158. Reading "qua formantur ad esse" (D) for "quae formantur ad esse" (M).

159. Adding "essentia vero res omnes facit quod sunt" (D).

160. Reading "Ad multas nos cogit" (D) for "Ad multas non cogit" (M).

161. See p. 62 above.

162. "mentem," viz. mind or wit.

163. Adding "Amplius, infundatur a parente quidlibet aliud, aut aliunde, sterile remanet et inutile quia secum non trahit vim animae" (D).

164. Below it is clear that souls do not come from a "root-stock," at least not as the "propagators of souls" understand it, that is not in the sense that the soul is divided when its nutritive power enters into the seed. See above pp. 76–77.

165. Reading "Dicit enim Solomon" (D) for "Dicit enim Salvator" (M).

166. That is, traducianists.

167. Although, it seems, only in a tropical sense.

168. Cf. *De peccato originali* 2, PL 160: 1078.

169. Reading "emittit" (D) for "enutrit" (M).

170. Adding "Totum est, nec latitudine diffunditur" (D).

171. Reading "Verum equidem est quia venit ab anima vis propagationis in semine" (D) for "Verum equidem est quia venit ab animalis propagatione in semine" (M).

172. Reading "verecundia animae" (D) for "reverentia animae" (M).

173. Reading "tota et plena et perfecta" (D) for "tota et plena perfecta" (M).

174. "in arte summa."

175. Reading "sic in essentiam" (D) for "sic essentiam" (M). For a fuller exposition of this theme, see also Odo's *Expositio in canonem missae*, PL 160: 1059D–1060B.

176. Reading "cum non sint omnes nisi una" (D) for "cum non sint omnes in una" (M).

177. "uniformis."

178. Reading "et suis efficientiis fiunt istae" (D) for "ut suis efficientiis fiant istae" (M).

179. Reading "a vivo corpore" (D) for "a suo corpore" (M).

180. Reading "Et herba caesa" (D) for "Et herba ipsa" (M).

181. Reading "ne me precor arguant fratres" (D) for "ne precor, arguant fratres" (M).

182. Reading "non potest mutari" (D) for "non potest muniri" (M).
183. Reading "levis" (D) for "lenis" (M).

A Disputation with the Jew, Leo, Concerning the Advent of Christ, the Son of God

1. Reading "abundantiore in confusione" (T) for "abundantiore infusione" (J, M).

2. "manente stylo." In antiquity a "stilus" or "stylus" was a writing instrument having one sharply pointed end and one broad, flat end. The pointed end of the stilus was used to trace letters upon wax tablets; the broad, flat end was used to smooth the wax, thereby erasing what had been written. Thus Cicero employs the phrase "stilum vertere" (cf. *Actio in Verrem* 2.2.41), lit. to turn the stilus, to suggest the act of erasure. Here Odo's phrase, "manente stylo," lit. with the stilus remaining in position, presumably with its pointed end applied to the wax, implies an indelible, unerasable quality. Consequently, if Acard thinks of his memory as analogous to a wax tablet, he is asking Odo to compose an argument so elegant and persuasive that it will be permanently inscribed upon it.

3. The council met on 18 November 1100.

4. A town in the Oise department of northern France.

5. The twelfth-century manuscripts (D) and (T) follow Odo's instructions, designating the speaker only by the letter "L" or "O." However (J), a fifteenth-century copy, provides the complete name for each speaker throughout the text, as does the printed edition in (M).

6. That is, about mid-afternoon, the ninth hour after dawn.

7. Reading "similiter" (D, T) for "singulariter" (M).

8. "ordinare."

9. Reading "opposuit" (D, T, and J) for "exposuit" (M).

10. "bono patientiae," lit. by the good of suffering.

11. Reading "quod prius non debebat, non enim debebat pati qui non peccaverat" (D, T, J) for "quo prius non debebat pati qui non peccaverat" (M).

12. This example is very near to one Anselm used, namely even a single look contrary to God's will. Cf. *Cur Deus Homo* 1.21.

13. Reading "nulla creatura liberare potest" (T).

14. The manuscripts (T) and (D) both omit the following clause in (M) and (J), "quam facere non poterat bonum, quod ante peccatum habebat." For that reason, I have omitted it as well.

15. Cf. *De peccato originali* 1, PL 160: 1071C.

16. Anselm replies to this complaint as well. See *Cur Deus Homo* 1.18. The solution, for him, lies in the claim that the number of men who will enter heaven will exceed the number of fallen angels, so that no man can be certain, or rejoice, that the fall of an angel has made his elevation possible.

17. Reading "fieret" (D, T) for "fuerat" (M, J). For a different contemporary view of why God wanted the number of the elect to consist of both men and angels, see Honorius, *Elucidarium* 1.26.

18. Reading "si bene superius comprehensa recolis" (D, T, J) for "si bene supernis comprehensa incolis" (M).

19. Reading "ideo necesse est ut utraeque naturae hominis et dei conveniant, et fiat Deus homo, et unus Jesus Christus Deus et homo, non alius Deus et alius homo, sed totus quicquid est deus est, et totus quicquid est homo est" (D, J) for "ideo necesse est ut utraeque naturae conveniant, et fiat Deus homo, et unus Jesus Christus Deus et homo, non alius Deus, et alius homo, sed totus quicquid est" (M, T).

20. Reading "nec ulla" (D, T, J) for "nec illa" (M).

21. Reading "non potes negare" (D, T, J) for "non potest negare" (M).

22. "praeponderet."

23. Reading "mors ergo ejus mala est ultra omnia. Est ergo mors Christi ultra omne peccatum" (D, T, J) for "mors ergo ejus mala est ultra omne peccatum" (M).

24. Sacrifice here is rendered by the Latin "hostia," a term which would have directed the reader also to the eucharistic host. For Odo, each time the eucharist is consecrated, it repeatedly offers the value of this original sacrificial death on the Cross and removes sin from those faithfully receiving it. Cf. *Expositio in canonem missae*, PL 160: 1064B–1065A.

25. Reading "sed debebat" (D, T, J) for "sed non debebat" (M).

26. Cf. *Cur Deus Homo* 1.3, where Boso, Anselm's interlocutor, complains that unbelievers often ridicule the Christian belief in the Virgin Birth as one that dishonors God. But Anselm's reply relies upon a theological notion of recapitulation. Odo's reply is more properly philosophical, appealing to divine omnipresence. For Odo's contribution to Christian-Jewish polemics on this point, see especially David Berger, *The Jewish-Christian Debate in the High Middle Ages* (Philadelphia: Jewish Publication Society, 1979), 350–351. For the role of the Virgin Birth in medieval Christian-Jewish polemics in general, see Bernhard Blumenkranz, *Juifs et Chrétiens dans le monde occidental 430–1096* (Paris: Mouton, 1960), 260–62; and Daniel Lasker, *Jewish Philosophical Polemics Against Christianity in the Middle Ages* (New York: KTAV Publishing House, 1977), 155–56.

27. Reading "Cum igitur nos implet" (D, T, J) for "Cum igitur non impleat" (M).

28. Boethius transmits a similar claim, noting that "reason convinces us that animate things, judged in the light of the quickening of the soul, should be preferred to inanimate things." See *Boethius's In Ciceronis Topica*, 174. The Latin text may be found in PL 64: 1161.

29. Cf. Augustine, *De libero arbitrio* 3.5.17.61–62, where the author expresses an almost identical sentiment.

30. Reading "secessum emittitur" (D) for "secessum dimittitur" (M).

31. Reading "luna" (D, T) for "lima."

32. This line is missing in (T).

33. Reading "purius" (D, T) for "plurius" (M). For Odo the mystery of the Virgin Birth has far-reaching implications. Because God can create a body for himself from the Virgin, he can also create flesh and blood for himself from the elements in the Eucharist. Cf. *Expositio in canonem missae*, PL 160: 1069A.

Bibliography

PRIMARY SOURCES

Aelred of Rievaulx, *Dialogus de anima*. In *Opera omnia*. Edited by A. Hoste and C.H. Talbot. CCCM, 1. Turnhout: Brepols, 1971.

———. *Dialogue on the Soul*. Translated by C.H. Talbot. Cistercian Fathers Series, no. 22. Kalamazoo, MI: Cistercian Publications, 1981.

Agobard of Lyon. *Liber contra objectiones Fredegisi abbatis*. PL 104: 159–174.

Albertus Magnus. *De natura et origine animae*. In *Opera omnia*, vol. 12. Edited by Bernhard Geyer. Cologne: Aschendorff, 1955.

Alcuin. *De dialectica*. PL 101: 949–976.

———. *Interrogationes et Responsiones in Genesim*. PL 100.

Amand du Chastel. *Amandus de Castello de Odonis episcopi Cameracensis vita vel moribus*. MGH, SS, 15, 2. Hanover, 1883; reprint, 1963. Pp. 942–945.

———. *Amandus de Castello de Odonis episcopi Cameracensis vita vel moribus*. In *Rouleaux des morts du XIe au XVe siècle*. Edited by Léopold Delisle. Paris: Librairie de la Société de l'Histoire de France, 1866. Pp. 171–177.

Anselm of Canterbury. *Opera omnia*. Edited by Francis Salesius Schmitt. 5 vols. Edinburgh: Thomas Nelson and Sons, 1946–51.

———. *Anselm of Canterbury*. Edited and translated by Jasper Hopkins. 4 vols. New York: Edwin Mellen Press, 1974–76.

Augustine. *De dialectica*. Translated by B. Darrell Jackson. Edited by Jan Pinborg. Dordrecht and Boston: D. Reidel Publishing Co., 1975.

———. *De diversis quaestionibus ad Simplicianum*. Edited by Almut Mutzenbecher. CCSL 44. Turnhout: Brepols, 1970.

———. *De libero arbitrio*. In *Opera*. Edited by W.M. Green. CCSL 29. Turnhout: Brepols, 1970.

———. *Enchiridion ad Laurentium*. Leipzig: Tauchnitii, 1838.

———. *Letters, IV (165–203)*. Translated by Sr. Wilfrid Parsons. The Fathers of the Church, 12. Washington, DC: Catholic University of America Press, 1964.

———. *On the Free Choice of the Will*. Translated with introduction and notes by Thomas Williams. Indianapolis: Hackett Publishing, 1993.

Berlière, Ursmer, editor. *De viris illustribus monasterii Sancti Martini Tornacensis*. In *Studien und Mittheilungen aus dem Benedictiner und dem Cistercienser Orden* 12(1891): 90–104.

Boethius. *Boethius's In Ciceronis Topica*. Translated by Eleonore Stump. Ithaca, NY: Cornell University Press, 1988.

——. *In Isagogen Porphyrii Commenta*. Edited by George Schepss. CSEL 48. Leipzig: 1906; reprint, New York: Johnson Reprint Co., 1966.

——. *Philosophiae Consolatio*. CCSL 94/1. Edited by Ludwig Bieler. Turnhout: Brepols, 1957.

——. *The Theological Tractates*. Translated by H.F. Stewart and E.K. Rand. London and New York: G.P. Putnam's Sons, 1918.

Cassiodorus. *De anima*. PL 70: 1279–1308.

Eadmer. *The Life of St. Anselm, Archbishop of Canterbury*. Edited by R.W. Southern. London: T. Nelson, 1962.

Fredigisus of Tours. *De nihil et tenebris*. PL 105: 751–756.

——. *Letter on Nothing and Darkness*. In *Medieval Philosophy from St. Augustine to Nicholas of Cusa*. Edited by John F. Wippel and Allan B. Wolter. New York: Free Press, 1969. Pp. 104–108.

Gesta Episcoporum Cameracensium. Edited by L.C. Bethmann. MGH, SS, 7, Hanover, 1846; reprint, 1968. Pp. 393–525.

Gesta Pontificum Cameracensium, Gestes des évêques de Cambrai de 1092 à 1138. Edited by Charles de Smedt. Paris: Société de l'Histoire de France, 1880.

Gerard of Cambrai. *Epistola Gerardi acta synodi Atrebatensis in Manichaeos*. PL 142.

Gilbert Crispin. *The Works of Gilbert Crispin Abbot of Westminster*. Edited by Anna Sapir Abulafia and G.R. Evans. London: Oxford University Press, 1989.

Gunzo. *Epistola ad Augienses*. Edited by Karl Manitius. MGH, Quellen zur Geistesgeschichte des Mittelalters, 2/1. Weimar: Hermann Böhlaus Nachfolger, 1958.

Herman of Tournai. *Herimanni Liber de restauratione monasterii Sancti Martini Tornacensis*. MGH, SS, 14. Hanover, 1883; reprint, 1963. Pp. 274–317.

Honorius. *L'élucidiarium et les lucidaires*. Edited by Yves Lefèvre. Bibliothèque des Écoles Françaises d'Athènes et de Rome, 124. Paris: Fayard, 1954.

Hugh of Ribemont. *Epistola ad G. Andegavensem*. PL 166: 833–36.

Isidore of Seville. *Etymologies Book II*. Edited and translated by Peter K. Marshall. Paris: Société d'Édition "Les Belles Lettres," 1983.

John of Salisbury. *The Metalogicon* (selection). In *Philosophy in the Middle Ages*. Edited by Arthur Hyman and James J. Walsh. Indianapolis: Hackett Publishing, 1977. Pp. 167–169.

Macrobius. *Commentarii in Somnium Scipionis*. Edited by Jacob Willis. Leipzig: Teubner, 1970.

Manegold of Lautenbach. *Liber Magistri Manigaldi contra Wolfelmum Coloniensem*. Edited by Wilfried Hartmann. MGH, Quellen zur Geistesgeschichte des Mittelalters, 8. Weimar: Bohlau, 1972.

Martianus Capella. *Martianus Capella and the Seven Liberal Arts*. Vol. 2: *The Marriage of Philology and Mercury*. Translated by William Harris Stahl and E.L. Burge. New York: Columbia University Press, 1977.

Odo of Tournai. *Opera omnia*. In *Maxima bibliotheca veterum patrum*. Edited by Maguerin de la Bigne. Vol. 21. Cologne: 1577.

——. *Opera omnia*. PL 160.

Odorannus of Sens. *Ad Everardum monachum, de tribus quaestionibus*. In *Opera omnia*. Edited by Robert-Henri Bautier, Monique Gilles, Marie-Elizabeth

Duchez, and Michel Hugo. Paris: Éditions du Centre National de la Recherche Scientifique, 1972.

Otloh of St. Emmeram. *Dialogus de tribus quaestionibus.* PL 146: 59–136.

Peter Abelard. "On Universals." In *Medieval Philosophy from St. Augustine to Nicholas of Cusa.* Edited by John F. Wippel and Allan B. Wolter. New York: Free Press, 1969. Pp. 190–203.

Peter Damian. *De tempore celebrandi nuptias.* PL 145.

———. *Lettre sur la toute-puissance divine.* Edited by André Cantin. Paris: Éditions du Cerf, 1972.

———. *Vita Romualdi.* Edited with introduction by Giovanni Tabacco. Fonti per la Storia d'Italia no. 94. Rome: Istituto Storico Italiano per il Medio Evo, 1957.

Peter Lombard. *Sententiae in IV libris distinctae.* 3rd edition. Spicilegium Bonaventurianum. Grottaferrata: 1971.

Porphyry. *Porphyry the Phoenician: Isagoge.* Translated with introduction and notes by Edward W. Warren. Toronto: Pontifical Institute of Mediaeval Studies, 1975.

Prudentius Clemens, Aurelius. *Works.* Vol. 1: *Carmen Apotheosis.* Edited and Translated by H.J. Thompson. Cambridge, MA: Harvard University Press, 1949.

Pseudo-Augustine. *Categoriae decem.* In *Aristoteles Latinus* 1.1–5; *Categoriae vel Praedicamenta.* Edited by L. Minio-Paluello. Bruges: Desclée de Brouwer, 1961. Pp. 133–175.

Rabanus Maurus. *Tractatus de anima.* PL 110: 1109–1119.

Ratramnus of Corbie. *Liber de anima ad Odonem Bellovacensem.* Edited by D.C. Lambot. Analecta Mediaevalia Namurcensia, 2. Namur: Centre d'Études Médiévales, 1951.

Robert Pullen. *Sententiarum libri octo.* PL 186: 726–732.

Rupert of Deutz. *De trinitate et operibus ejus: In Gen.* PL 167.

Simon of Tournai. *Les Disputationes de Simon de Tournai.* Edited by Joseph Warichez. Spicilegium Sacrum Lovaniense, Études et Documents, 12. Louvain: 1932.

Werner of St. Blaise. *Deflorationes SS. Patrum 2: De origine animae.* PL 157.

SECONDARY SOURCES

Abulafia, Anna Sapir. "An Eleventh-Century Exchange of Letters Between a Christian and a Jew." *Journal of Medieval History* 7(1981): 153–174.

———. "Jewish-Christian Disputations and the Twelfth-Century Renaissance." *Journal of Medieval History* 15(1989): 105–125.

Amann, Émile. "Odon de Cambrai." *Dictionnaire de Théologie Catholique* 11: 932–935.

"Ancienne abbatiale Saint-Martin." *Dictionnaire des Églises de France* 5: 127–128.

Auger, A. "Odon de Cambrai." *Biographie Nationale (de Belgique).* Brussels: H. Thiry van Buggenhoudt, 1866–1986. 16: 75–78.

Balboni, Dante. "San Pier Damiano, Maestro e Discepolo in Pomposa." *Benedictina* 22(1975): 73–89.

Barach, Carl Sigmund. "Zur Geschichte des Nominalismus vor Roscellin." In *Kleine Philosophische Schriften*. Vienna: Wilhelm Braumüller, 1878. Pp. 5–25.

Bazàn, Bernardo C. *Les questions disputées*. In *Les questions disputées et les questions quodlibétiques dans les facultés de théologie, de droit et de médicine*, fasc. 44–45. Typologie des Sources du Moyen Âge Occidental. Turnhout: Brepols, 1985. Pp. 21–149.

Becquet, Jean. "L'érémitisme clérical et laïc dans l'Ouest de la France." In *L'eremitismo in Occidente nei secoli XI e XII. Atti della settimana internazionale di studio.* Milan: Miscellanea del Centro di Studi Medioevali 4, 1965. Pp. 182–211.

Benson, Robert L. and Giles Constable, editors. *Renaissance and Renewal in the Twelfth Century*. Cambridge, MA: Harvard University Press, 1982.

Berger, David. *The Jewish-Christian Debate in the High Middle Ages*. Philadelphia: Jewish Publication Society, 1979.

Berlière, Ursmer. *Monasticon Belge*. Liège: Centre National de Recherches d'Histoire Religieuse, 1964. 4/1–3: 692–93; 725.

———. *Monasticon Belge*. Abbaye de Maredsous, 1897. 1/a.

Berteaux, Ernest. *Étude historique de Cambrai, 500–1798*. 2 vols. Cambrai: impr. d'Halluin-Carlon, 1908.

Bibliotheca Hagiographica Latina antiquae et mediae aetatis. Edited by the Socii Bollandiani. 2 vols. Brussels: Socii Bollandiani, 1898–1901.

Blachère, François de Paule. "La péché originel d'après Saint Anselme." *Revue Augustinienne* 6(1905): 241–255.

Blumenkranz, Bernhard. *Juifs et Chrétiens dans le monde occidental 430–1096*. Paris: Mouton, 1960.

———. "Jüdische und christliche Konvertiten im jüdische-christlichen Religionsgespräch des Mittelalters." In *Judentum im Mittelalter: Beiträge zum christlich-jüdischen Gespräch*. Edited by Paul Wilpert and Willehad Paul Eckert. Miscellanea Mediaevalia, 4. Berlin: De Gruyter, 1966. Pp. 264–282.

Blumenthal, Uta-Renate. *The Early Councils of Pope Paschal II, 1100–1110*. Toronto: Pontifical Institute of Mediaeval Studies, 1978.

Boutemy, André. "Odon d'Orléans et les origines de la bibliothèque de l'abbaye de Saint-Martin de Tournai." *Mélanges dédiés à la mémoire de Félix Grat*. 2 vols. Paris: Mme. Pecquer-Grat, 1946–49. 2: 179–223.

Browe, Peter. *Die Judenmission im Mittelalter und die Päpste*. Miscellanea Historiae Pontificiae, 6. Rome: Università Gregoriana, 1973.

Bynum, Caroline Walker. *Docere Verbo et Exemplo. An Aspect of Twelfth Century Spirituality*. Missoula, MT: Scholars Press, 1979.

Cadden, Joan. *Meanings of Sex Difference in the Middle Ages*. Cambridge: Cambridge University Press, 1993.

Cantor, Norman. "The Crisis of Western Monasticism, 1050–1130." *American Historical Review* 66(1960): 47–61.

Cauchie, Alfred. *La querelle des investitures dans les diocèses de Liège et de Cambrai*, par. 2. Louvain: Charles Peeters, 1891.

Ceillier, Rémy. "Odon, Évêque de Cambrai." *Histoire Générale des Auteurs Sacrés et Ecclésiastiques*. Paris: L. Vives, 1858–63. 14/1: 68–77.

Chartier, M. "Cambrai." *Dictionnaire d'Histoire et de Géographie Ecclésiastiques.* Edited by Alfred Baudrillart et al. Paris: Letouzey et Ane, 1912–. 11: 547–565.

Châtillon, Jean. "La crise de l'Église aux XIᵉ et XIIᵉ siècles et les origines des grandes fédérations canoniales." *Revue d'Histoire de la Spiritualité* 53(1977): 3–46.

Chenu, M.D. *Nature, Man, and Society in the Twelfth Century.* Translated by Jerome Taylor and Lester K. Little. Chicago: University of Chicago Press, 1968.

Colish, Marcia L. "Carolingian Debates over *Nihil* and *Tenebrae*: A Study in Theological Method." *Speculum* 59/4(1984): 757–795.

Corvino, Francesco. "Il 'de nihilo et tenebris' di Fredegiso di Tours." *Revista Critica di Storia della Filosofia* 47(1956): 273–286.

Courtenay, William J. "Nominalism and Late Medieval Thought: A Bibliographical Essay." *Theological Studies* 33(1972): 716–734. Reprinted in *Covenant and Causality in Medieval Thought.* London: Variorum Reprints, 1984.

Da Cruz Pontes, J.M. "Le problème de l'origine de l'âme de la patristique à la solution thomiste." *Recherches de Théologie Ancienne et Médiévale* 31(1964): 175–229.

Dahan, Gilbert. *Les intellectuels chrétiens et les juifs au moyen âge.* Paris: Éditions du Cerf, 1990.

Daly, Grabriel. "Theological Models in the Doctrine of Original Sin." *Heythrop Journal* 13(1972): 121–142.

De Clerck, D.E. "Questions de sotériologie médiévale." *Recherches de Théologie Médiévale* 13(1946): 150–184.

Delaruelle, Étienne. "Les ermites et spiritualité populaire." In *L'eremitismo in Occidente nei secoli XI e XII. Atti della settimana internazionale di studio.* Milan: Miscellanea del Centro di Studi Medioevali 4, 1965. Pp. 212–247.

Dereine, Charles. "Chanoines." *Dictionnaire d'Historie et de Géographie Ecclésiastiques.* Edited by Alfred Baudrillart et al. Paris: Letouzey et Ane, 1912–. 12: 350–405.

———. "Ermites, reclus et recluses dans l'ancien diocèse de Cambrai entre Scarpe et Haine (1075–1125)." *Revue Bénédictine* 97(1987): 289–313.

———. "Odon de Tournai et la crise du cénobitisme au XIᵉ siècle." *Revue du Moyen Âge Latin* 4(1948): 137–154.

De Rijk, L. M. *Logica modernorum.* 2 vols. Assen: Van Gorcum, 1962–67.

Destombes, C.J. "La tradition des églises de Cambrai et d'Arras." *Revue des Sciences Ecclésiastiques* 4(1861): 116–121.

De Wulf, Maurice. *Histoire de la philosophie médiévale.* 6th edition. Louvain: Institut Superieur de Philosophie, 1934.

D'Haenens, Albert. *L'Abbaye Saint-Martin de Tournai de 1290 à 1350.* Louvain: Publications Universitaires Louvain, 1961.

———. "Moines et clercs à Tournai au début du XIIᵉ siècle." In *La vita comune del clero nei secoli XI e XII, atti della Settimana di studio: Mendola, settembre 1959.* 2 vols. Milan: Miscellanea del Centro di Studi Medioevali 3, 1959. 2:90–103.

Dickinson, J.L. "Canons Regular of St. Augustine." *New Catholic Encyclopedia* 3: 62–64.

Dubois, Jean-Marie. "Transmission et rémission du péché originel. Genèse de la réflexion théologique de saint Thomas d'Aquin." *Revue des études augustiniennes* 29(1983): 283–311.

Erdmann, Johann Eduard. *A History of Philosophy*. Translated by Williston S. Hough. 2 vols. London and New York: Macmillan Co., 1910.

Ewbank, W.F. "Anselm, on Sin and Atonement." *Church Quarterly Review* 146 (1948): 61–67.

Fairweather, Eugene Rathbone. *A Scholastic Miscellany: Anselm to Ockham*. Philadelphia: Westminster Press, 1956.

Gold, Penny S. "The Marriage of Mary and Joseph in the Twelfth-Century Ideology of Marriage." In *Sexual Practices and the Medieval Church*. Edited by Vern Bullough and James Brundage. Buffalo, NY: Prometheus Books, 1982. Pp. 102–117.

Grabmann, Martin. *Die Geschichte der scholastischen Methode*. Berlin: Akademie-Verlag, 1956.

Green, Monica H. "Constantinus Africanus and the Conflict between Religion and Science." In *The Human Embryo: Aristotle and the Arabic and European Traditions*. Edited by G.R. Dunstan. Exeter: University of Exeter Press, 1990. Pp. 47–69.

Gregory, Tullio. *Platonismo medievale*. Studi Storici, fasc. 26–28. Rome: Istituto Storico Italiano per il Medio Evo, 1958.

Gross, Julius. *Geschichte des Erbsündendogmas*. Vol. 3: *Entwicklungsgeschichte des Erbsündendogmas im Zeitalter der Scholastik (12.–15. Jahrhundert)*. Basel and Munich: Ernst Reinhart Verlag, 1971.

Hartmanm, Wilfried. "Manegold von Lautenbach und die Anfänge der Frühscholastik." *Deutsches Archiv für Erforschung des Mittelalters* 26(1970): 47–149.

Hauréau, Blaise. *Histoire de la philosophie scolastique*. Paris: Durand et Pedone-Lauriel, 1872.

Heaney, Seamus P. *The Development of the Sacramentality of Marriage from Anselm of Laon to Thomas Aquinas*. Catholic University of America Studies in Sacred Theology, 2nd ser., no. 134, Washington, DC: Catholic University of America Press, 1963.

Hopkins, Jasper. *A Companion to the Study of St. Anselm*. Minneapolis: University of Minnesota Press, 1972.

Huby, Pamela M. "Soul, Life, Sense, Intellect: Some Thirteenth-Century Problems." In *The Human Embryo: Aristotle and the Arabic and European Traditions*. Edited by G.R. Dunstan. Exeter: University of Exeter Press, 1990. Pp. 113–122.

Hulen, Amos B. "The 'Dialogues with the Jews' as Sources for the Early Jewish Argument Against Christianity." *Journal of Biblical Literature* 5(1932): 58–70.

Huyghebaert, Nicolas. "Les femmes laïques dans la vie religieuse des XIᵉ et XIIᵉ siècles dans la province ecclésiastique du Reims." In *I Laici nella " 'Societas Christiana" dei secoli XI e XII*. Milan: Miscellanea del Centro di Studi Medioevali 5, 1965. Pp. 346–395.

Hyman, Arthur and James J. Walsh, editors. *Philosophy in the Middle Ages*. Indianapolis: Hackett Publishing Co., 1977.

Kelly, J.N.D. *Early Christian Doctrines*. 5th ed. rev. New York: Harper and Row, 1978.

Labis, F.J. "Le bienheureaux Odon, évêque du Cambrai." *Revue Catholique de Louvain* 14(1856): 445–460; 519–526; 574–585.

Lasker, Daniel. *Jewish Philosophical Polemics Against Christianity in the Middle Ages.* New York: KTAV Publishing House, 1977.

———. *"Qiṣṣat Mujādalat al-Usquf* and *Nestor Ha-Komer.* The Earliest Arabic and Hebrew Jewish anti-Christian Polemics." In *Genizah Research After Ninety Years: The Case of Judeo-Arabic.* Edited by J. Blau and S.C. Reif. Cambridge: Cambridge University Press, 1992. Pp. 112–118.

Lebreton, M.M. "Recherches sur les manuscrits des sermons de différents personnages du XIIᵉ siècle nommés Odon." *Bulletin d'Information de l'Institut de Recherche et d'Histoire des Textes* 3(1955): 33–54.

Leclercq, Jean. "'Eremus' et 'eremita.' Pour l'histoire du vocabulaire de la vie solitaire." *Collectanea Ordinis Cisterciensis Reformatorum* 25(1963): 8–30.

———. "The Monastic Crisis of the Eleventh and Twelfth Centuries." In *Cluniac Monasticism in the Central Middle Ages.* Edited by Noreen Hunt. Hamden, CT: Archon Books, 1971. Pp. 217–237.

———. "Odo von Cambrai." *Lexikon für Theologie und Kirche.* Edited by Josef Hofer and Karl Rahner. Freiburg: Herder, 1957–65. 7: 1099.

———. "La spiritualité des chanoines réguliers." In *La vita comune del clero nei secoli XI e XII, atti della Settimana di studio: Mendola, settembre 1959.* 2 vols. Milan: Miscellanea del Centro di Studi Medioevali 3, 1959. 1: 117–135.

Leyser, Henrietta. *Hermits and the New Monasticism: A Study of Religious Communities in Western Europe 1000–1150.* New York: St. Martin's Press, 1984.

Lottin, Odon. *Psychologie et morale aux XIIᵉ et XIIIᵉ siècles.* 8 volumes in 4. Louvain: Abbaye du Mont César, 1942–1954.

Lyon, Bryce. "Commune." *Dictionary of the Middle Ages* 3: 493–503.

Lyonnet, S. "Le péché originel et le exégèse de Rom. 5, 12–14." *Recherches de Science Religieuse* 44(1956): 63–84.

Manitius, Max. *Geschichte der lateinische Literatur des Mittelalters.* 3 vols. Munich: C.H. Beck, 1911–1931.

Marenbon, John. *From the Circle of Alcuin to the School of Auxerre: Logic, Theology, and Philosophy in the Early Middle Ages.* Cambridge: Cambridge University Press, 1981.

Martin, Raymond M. "La question du péché originel dans Saint Anselme (1099–1100)." *Revue des Sciences Philosophiques et Théologiques* 5(1911): 735–749.

Michel, A. "Justice originelle." *Dictionnaire de théologie Catholique* 8:2020–2042.

———. "Traducianisme." *Dictionnaire de théologie Catholique* 15:1351–1366.

Milis, Ludo. "Ermites et chanoines réguliers au XIIᵉ siècle." *Cahiers de Civilisation Médiévale* 22(1979): 39–80.

"Monumenta Historiae Tornacensis." In MGH, SS, 14. Hanover, 1883; reprint, 1963. Pp. 266–273.

Naedenoen, Paul. "Odon de Cambrai: Traité sur le canon de la Messe." Thesis. Université Catholique de Louvain: Institut Supérior des Sciences Religieuses, 1969.

Obermann, Heiko A. *"Via Antiqua* and *Via Moderna*: Late Medieval Prolegomena to Early Reformation Thought." *Journal of the History of Ideas* 48(1987): 23–40.

O'Connell, R.J. "The Origin of the Soul in St. Augustine's Letter 143." *Revue des Études Augustiniennes* 28(1982): 239–52.

————. *The Origin of the Soul in St. Augustine's Later Works*. New York: Fordham University Press, 1987.

O'Daly, Gerard. *Augustine's Philosophy of Mind*. London: Duckworth, 1987.

"Odon, Évêque de Cambray." *Bibliothéque Générale des Écrivains de l'Ordre de S. Benoît*. Edited by J. François. Bouillion: 1777–1778. 4 vols., reprint; Louvain-Héverlé: 1961. 2: 346–348.

Pelikan, Jaroslav. *The Christian Tradition: A History of Development and Doctrine*. Vol. 1: *The Emergence of the Catholic Tradition (100–600)*. Chicago: University of Chicago Press, 1971.

Phipps, Colin. "Romuald, Model Hermit. Eremitical Theory in Saint Peter Damian's 'Vita Beati Romualdi,' chapters 16–27." In *Monks, Hermits, and the Ascetic Tradition*. Edited by W.J. Sheils. Studies in Church History 22. Ecclesiastical History Society. Oxford: B. Blackwell, 1985. Pp. 65–77.

Picavet, François. *Roscelin, philosophe et théologien*. Paris: Félix Alcan, 1911.

Platelle, Henri. "La mort précieuse: La mort des moines d'après quelques sources des Pays Bas du sud." *Revue Mabillon* 60(1982): 150–160; 161–173.

Purday, K.M. "Berengar and the Use of the Word *Substantia*." *Downside Review* 91(1973): 101–110.

Pycke, Jacques. *Le chapitre cathédral Notre-Dame de Tournai de la fin du XIᵉ à la fin du XIIIᵉ siècle*. Recueil de Travaux d'Histoire et de Philologie 6, 30. Brussels: Université de Louvain, 1986.

Reiners, Joseph. *Der Nominalismus in der Frühscholastik: Ein Beitrag zur Geschichte der Universalienfrage im Mittelalter*. Münster: Aschendorff, 1910.

Rembaum, Joel E. "Medieval Jewish Criticism of the Christian Doctrine of Original Sin." *Association for Jewish Studies* 7–8(1982–83): 353–382.

Resnick, Irven M. "Attitudes Toward Philosophy and Dialectic During the Gregorian Reform." *Journal of Religious History* 16/2(1990): 115–125.

————. "*Lingua Dei, lingua hominis*: Sacred Language and Medieval Texts." *Viator* 21(1990): 51–74.

————. "Odo of Tournai and Peter Damian: Poverty and Crisis in the Eleventh Century." *Revue Bénédictine* 98, 1/2 (1988): 114–40.

————. "Odo of Tournai's *De peccato originali* and the Problem of Original Sin." *Medieval Philosophy and Theology* 1(1991): 18–38.

————. "Peter Damian on Cluny, Liturgy, and Penance." *Journal of Religious History* 15/1(1988): 61–75. Reprinted in *Studia Liturgica* 18/2(1988): 170–187.

————. "*Risus monasticus*: Laughter and Medieval Monastic Culture." *Revue Bénédictine* 97, 1/2 (1987): 90–100.

Reuther, Rosemary Radford. *Faith and Fratricide: The Theological Roots of Anti-Semitism*. New York: Seabury Press, 1974.

Rokéah, David. "The Church Fathers and the Jews in Writings Designed for Internal and External Use." In *Antisemitism Through the Ages*. Edited by Shmuel Almog. Oxford: Pergamon Press, 1988. Pp. 39–70.

Rondet, Henri. *Le péché originel dans la tradition patristique et théologique*. Fayard: 1967.

Roques, René. "La méthode de Saint Anselme dans le 'Cur Deus Homo'." *Aquinas. Ephemerides Thomisticae* 5(1962): 3–57.

Russell, Jeffrey Burton. "A propos du synode d'Arras, en 1025." *Revue d'Histoire Ecclésiastique* 57(1962): 66–87.

———. *Dissent and Reform in the Early Middle Ages*. Berkeley and Los Angeles: University of California Press, 1965.

Schaefer, Mary M. "Twelfth Century Latin Commentaries on the Mass: The Relationship of the Priest to Christ and to the People." *Studia Liturgica* 15(1982–83): 76–86.

"Senlis." *Encyclopaedia Judaica* 14: 1161.

Sheets, John H. "Justice in the Moral Thought of St. Anselm." *Modern Schoolman* 25(1948): 132–139.

Smith, Aloysius. "Chanoines réguliers." *Dictionnaire de Spiritualité* 2: 463–477.

Stannard, Jerry. *Selected Medieval Garden Plants and Their Uses*. Lawrence: University of Kansas Press, 1983.

Tabacco, Giovanni. "Romualdo di Ravenna e gli inizi dell'eremitismo camaldolese." In *L'eremitismo in Occidente nei secoli XI e XII. Atti della settimana internazionale di studio*. Milan: Miscellanea del Centro di Studi Medioevali, 4, 1965. Pp. 73–121.

Teske, Roland. "Review of R.J. O'Connell's *The Origin of the Soul in St. Augustine's Later Works*." *The Modern Schoolman* 66/1 (1988): 71–78.

"Titles of Nobility." *Encyclopaedia Judaica* 15: 1165–1166.

Tolan, E.K. "John of Salisbury and the Problem of Medieval Humanism." In *Études d'Histoire Littéraire et Doctrinale*, 4th ser. 19. Montréal: Institut d'Études Médiévales, 1968. Pp. 189–199.

Toner, P.J. "St. Anselm's Definition of Original Sin." *Irish Theological Quarterly* 3(1908): 425–436.

"Tournai." *Dictionnaire des Églises de France* 5: 120–127.

Van de Vyver, A. "Les étapes du développement philosophique du haut moyen-age." *Revue Belge de Philologie et d'Histoire* 8(1929): 425–452.

Van den Broek, R. *The Myth of the Phoenix According to Classical and Early Christian Traditions*. Leiden: E.J. Brill, 1972.

Van Engen, John. "The 'Crisis of Cenobitism' Reconsidered. Benedictine Monasticism in the Years 1050–1150." *Speculum* 61(1986): 269–304.

———. *Rupert of Deutz*. Berkeley: University of California Press, 1983.

Williams, John R. "Godfrey of Rheims, a Humanist of the Eleventh Century." *Speculum* 22(1947): 29–45.

Wilmart, André, editor. *Bibliothecae Apostolicae Vaticanae: Codices Reginenses Latini*. Vol. 2: *Codices 251–500*. Vatican: Bibliotheca Vaticana, 1945.

Wippel, John F. and Allan B. Wolter, eds. *Medieval Philosophy from St. Augustine to Nicholas of Cusa*. New York: Free Press, 1969.

Index to Biblical Passages Cited

General Index

University of Pennsylvania Press
MIDDLE AGES SERIES
Edward Peters, General Editor

F. R. P. Akehurst, trans. *The* Coutumes de Beauvaisis *of Philippe de Beaumanoir*. 1992
Peter L. Allen. *The Art of Love: Amatory Fiction from Ovid to the* Romance of the Rose. 1992
David Anderson. *Before the Knight's Tale: Imitation of Classical Epic in Boccaccio's* Teseida. 1988
Benjamin Arnold. *Count and Bishop in Medieval Germany: A Study of Regional Power, 1100–1350*. 1991
Mark C. Bartusis. *The Late Byzantine Army: Arms and Society, 1204–1453*. 1992
J. M. W. Bean. *From Lord to Patron: Lordship in Late Medieval England*. 1990
Uta-Renate Blumenthal. *The Investiture Controversy: Church and Monarchy from the Ninth to the Twelfth Century*. 1988
Daniel Bornstein, trans. *Dino Compagni's* Chronicle *of Florence*. 1986
Maureen Boulton. *The Song in the Story: Lyric Insertions in French Narrative Fiction, 1200–1400*. 1993
Betsy Bowden. *Chaucer Aloud: The Varieties of Textual Interpretation*. 1987
Charles R. Bowlus. *Franks, Moravians, and Magyars: The Struggle for the Middle Danube, 788–907*. 1994
James William Brodman. *Ransoming Captives in Crusader Spain: The Order of Merced on the Christian-Islamic Frontier*. 1986
Kevin Brownlee and Sylvia Huot, eds. *Rethinking the* Romance of the Rose*: Text, Image, Reception*. 1992
Matilda Tomaryn Bruckner. *Shaping Romance: Interpretation, Truth, and Closure in Twelfth-Century French Fictions*. 1993
Otto Brunner (Howard Kaminsky and James Van Horn Melton, eds. and trans.). Land *and Lordship: Structures of Governance in Medieval Austria*. 1992
Robert I. Burns. S.J., ed. *Emperor of Culture: Alfonso X the Learned of Castile and His Thirteenth-Century Renaissance*. 1990
David Burr. *Olivi and Franciscan Poverty: The Origins of the* Usus Pauper *Controversy*. 1989
David Burr. *Olivi's Peaceable Kingdom: A Reading of the Apocalypse Commentary*. 1993
Thomas Cable. *The English Alliterative Tradition*. 1991
Anthony K. Cassell and Victoria Kirkham, eds. and trans. *Diana's Hunt/Caccia di Diana: Boccaccio's First Fiction*. 1991
John C. Cavadini. *The Last Christology of the West: Adoptionism in Spain and Gaul, 785–820*. 1993
Brigitte Cazelles. *The Lady as Saint: A Collection of French Hagiographic Romances of the Thirteenth Century*. 1991

Karen Cherewatuk and Ulrike Wiethaus, eds. *Dear Sister: Medieval Women and the Epistolary Genre.* 1993

Anne L. Clark. *Elisabeth of Schönau: A Twelfth-Century Visionary.* 1992

Willene B. Clark and Meradith T. McMunn, eds. *Beasts and Birds of the Middle Ages: The Bestiary and Its Legacy.* 1989

Richard C. Dales. *The Scientific Achievement of the Middle Ages.* 1973

Charles T. Davis. *Dante's Italy and Other Essays.* 1984

Katherine Fischer Drew, trans. *The Burgundian Code.* 1972

Katherine Fischer Drew, trans. *The Laws of the Salian Franks.* 1991

Katherine Fischer Drew, trans. *The Lombard Laws.* 1973

Nancy Edwards. *The Archaeology of Early Medieval Ireland.* 1990

Margaret J. Ehrhart. *The Judgment of the Trojan Prince Paris in Medieval Literature.* 1987

Richard K. Emmerson and Ronald B. Herzman. *The Apocalyptic Imagination in Medieval Literature.* 1992

Theodore Evergates. *Feudal Society in Medieval France: Documents from the County of Champagne.* 1993

Felipe Fernández-Armesto. *Before Columbus: Exploration and Colonization from the Mediterranean to the Atlantic, 1229–1492.* 1987

Jerold C. Frakes. *Brides and Doom: Gender, Property, and Power in Medieval Women's Epic.* 1994

R. D. Fulk. *A History of Old English Meter.* 1992

Patrick J. Geary. *Aristocracy in Provence: The Rhône Basin at the Dawn of the Carolingian Age.* 1985

Peter Heath. *Allegory and Philosophy in Avicenna (Ibn Sînâ), with a Translation of the Book of the Prophet Muḥammad's Ascent to Heaven.* 1992

J. N. Hillgarth, ed. *Christianity and Paganism, 350–750: The Conversion of Western Europe.* 1986

Richard C. Hoffmann. *Land, Liberties, and Lordship in a Late Medieval Countryside: Agrarian Structures and Change in the Duchy of Wrocław.* 1990

Robert Hollander. *Boccaccio's Last Fiction: Il Corbaccio.* 1988

Edward B. Irving, Jr. *Rereading* Beowulf. 1989

C. Stephen Jaeger. *The Envy of Angels: Cathedral Schools and Social Ideals in Medieval Europe, 950–1200.* 1994

C. Stephen Jaeger. *The Origins of Courtliness: Civilizing Trends and the Formation of Courtly Ideals, 939–1210.* 1985

William Chester Jordan. *The French Monarchy and the Jews: From Philip Augustus to the Last Capetians.* 1989

William Chester Jordan. *From Servitude to Freedom: Manumission in the Sénonais in the Thirteenth Century.* 1986

Donald J. Kagay, trans. *The Usatges of Barcelona: The Fundamental Law of Catalonia.* 1994

Richard Kay. *Dante's Christian Astrology.* 1994

Ellen E. Kittell. *From Ad Hoc to Routine: A Case Study in Medieval Bureaucracy.* 1991

Alan C. Kors and Edward Peters, eds. *Witchcraft in Europe, 1100–1700: A Documentary History.* 1972

Barbara M. Kreutz. *Before the Normans: Southern Italy in the Ninth and Tenth Centuries*. 1992

E. Ann Matter. *The Voice of My Beloved: The Song of Songs in Western Medieval Christianity*. 1990

A. J. Minnis. *Medieval Theory of Authorship*. 1988

Lawrence Nees. *A Tainted Mantle: Hercules and the Classical Tradition at the Carolingian Court*. 1991

Lynn H. Nelson, trans. *The Chronicle of San Juan de la Peña: A Fourteenth-Century Official History of the Crown of Aragon*. 1991

Joseph F. O'Callaghan. *The Cortes of Castile-León, 1188–1350*. 1989

Joseph F. O'Callaghan. *The Learned King: The Reign of Alfonso X of Castile*. 1993

Odo of Tournai (Irven M. Resnick, trans.). On Original Sin *and* A Disputation with the Jew, Leo, Concerning the Advent of Christ, the Son of God: *Two Theological Treatises*. 1994

David M. Olster. *Roman Defeat, Christian Response, and the Literary Construction of the Jew*. 1994

William D. Paden, ed. *The Voice of the Trobairitz: Perspectives on the Women Troubadours*. 1989

Edward Peters. *The Magician, the Witch, and the Law*. 1982

Edward Peters, ed. *Christian Society and the Crusades, 1198–1229: Sources in Translation, including* The Capture of Damietta *by Oliver of Paderborn*. 1971

Edward Peters, ed. *The First Crusade: The* Chronicle *of Fulcher of Chartres and Other Source Materials*. 1971

Edward Peters, ed. *Heresy and Authority in Medieval Europe*. 1980

James M. Powell. *Albertanus of Brescia: The Pursuit of Happiness in the Early Thirteenth Century*. 1992

James M. Powell. *Anatomy of a Crusade, 1213–1221*. 1986

Susan A. Rabe. *Faith, Art, and Politics at Saint-Riquier: The Symbolic Vision of Angilbert*. 1994

Jean Renart (Patricia Terry and Nancy Vine Durling, trans.). *The Romance of the Rose or Guillaume de Dole*. 1993

Michael Resler, trans. Erec *by Hartmann von Aue*. 1987

Pierre Riché (Michael Idomir Allen, trans.). *The Carolingians: A Family Who Forged Europe*. 1993

Pierre Riché (Jo Ann McNamara, trans.). *Daily Life in the World of Charlemagne*. 1988

Jonathan Riley-Smith. *The First Crusade and the Idea of Crusading*. 1986

Joel T. Rosenthal. *Patriarchy and Families of Privilege in Fifteenth-Century England*. 1991

Teofilo F. Ruiz. *Crisis and Continuity: Land and Town in Late Medieval Castile*. 1994

Steven D. Sargent, ed. and trans. *On the Threshold of Exact Science: Selected Writings of Anneliese Maier on Late Medieval Natural Philosophy*. 1982

Robin Chapman Stacey. *The Road to Judgment: From Custom to Court in Medieval Ireland and Wales*. 1994

Sarah Stanbury. *Seeing the* Gawain-*Poet: Description and the Act of Perception*. 1992

Robert D. Stevick. *The Earliest Irish and English Bookart: Visual and Poetic Forms Before A.D. 1000.* 1994

Thomas C. Stillinger. *The Song of Troilus: Lyric Authority in the Medieval Book.* 1992

Susan Mosher Stuard. *A State of Deference: Ragusa/Dubrovnik in the Medieval Centuries.* 1992

Susan Mosher Stuard, ed. *Women in Medieval History and Historiography.* 1987

Susan Mosher Stuard, ed. *Women in Medieval Society.* 1976

Jonathan Sumption. *The Hundred Years War: Trial by Battle.* 1992

Ronald E. Surtz. *The Guitar of God: Gender, Power, and Authority in the Visionary World of Mother Juana de la Cruz (1481–1534).* 1990

William H. TeBrake. *A Plague of Insurrection: Popular Politics and Peasant Revolt in Flanders, 1323–1328.* 1993

Patricia Terry, trans. *Poems of the Elder Edda.* 1990

Hugh M. Thomas. *Vassals, Heiresses, Crusaders, and Thugs: The Gentry of Angevin Yorkshire, 1154–1216.* 1993

Ralph V. Turner. *Men Raised from the Dust: Administrative Service and Upward Mobility in Angevin England.* 1988

Mary F. Wack. *Lovesickness in the Middle Ages: The* Viaticum *and Its Commentaries.* 1990

Benedicta Ward. *Miracles and the Medieval Mind: Theory, Record, and Event, 1000–1215.* 1982

Suzanne Fonay Wemple. *Women in Frankish Society: Marriage and the Cloister, 500–900.* 1981

Jan M. Ziolkowski. *Talking Animals: Medieval Latin Beast Poetry, 750–1150.* 1993